COPY 28

Shahane, Vasant Anant, 1923-
Rudyard Kipling: activist and artist
[by] Vasant A. Shahane. With a pref. by
Harry T. Moore. Carbondale, Southern
Illinois University Press [1973]
xiii, 157 p. Bibl.
(Crosscurrents/modern critiques) 6.95

1. Kipling, Rudyard, 1865-1936.

Crosscurrents / MODERN CRITIQUES

Harry T. Moore, *General Editor*

RUDYARD KIPLING
Activist and Artist

Vasant A. Shahane

WITH A PREFACE BY

Harry T. Moore

SOUTHERN ILLINOIS UNIVERSITY PRESS
Carbondale and Edwardsville

FEFFER & SIMONS, INC.
London and Amsterdam

For
Neelima and Deepak

Library of Congress Cataloging in Publication Data

Shahane, Vasant Anant, 1923–
    Rudyard Kipling: activist and artist.

    (Crosscurrents/modern critiques)
    Bibliography: p.
    1. Kipling, Rudyard, 1865–1936.
PR4856.S47   828'.8'09   73–9536
ISBN 0–8093–0622–0

Contents

Rudyard Kipling: to many of us that name brings back
memories of reading in childhood (or being read to), and
of the poet whose jingoistic rhymes jingled wonderfully.
After we grew up, many of us no longer succumbed to the
cadences of "Mandalay," "Gunga Din," "Danny Deever,"
and the others. We had learned about Empire, and hadn't
liked what we learned.

Yet the charm of Puck of Pook's Hill couldn't be shaken
away, and the iron march of those soldiers in all the Roman-
army stories remained with us like pulse beats—and how
right Edmund Wilson seemed when he spoke of the enduring excellence of those tales. But Kipling seemed to most
of us only a minor and dated author.

It was a bit of a shock to find J. I. M. Stewart, in 1963,
in Eight Modern Writers (the twelfth volume of the Oxford History of English Literature Series), discussing Kipling
seriously along with Joyce, Lawrence, Henry James, and a
few others we considered the authors of stature. But those
of us who have enjoyed the surprises Mr. Stewart provides
under the pen name of Michael Innes shouldn't have been
too crushingly overcome by astonishment. The odd part of
the experience was that, without stretching the odds, Mr.
Stewart quietly and implicitly made out for Kipling what
is usually called a good case. And there were other serious
writers who dealt with Kipling as a serious writer, for example that very fine critic Bonamy Dobrée. Of course we
knew that T. S. Eliot had earlier even prepared an anthology

of Kipling's poems and written a long and friendly introduction to them; but we shrugged this off as the regrettable Establishment side of Eliot.

But he unabashedly kept up his praise of Kipling, notably when he addressed the Kipling Society in 1959: "I suggest that the fact that Kipling was an intuitive and not an intellectual, may go to his being underrated by intellectuals who are not intuitives." He boldly added, "He seems to me the greatest English man of letters of his generation." Approbation from Sir Hubert, indeed.

Well, I remain one who isn't "sold" on the poetry, though I now like most of the stories, beginning with Plain Tales from the Hills. Puck of Pook's Hill remains a warm memory, and those Roman-legion stories still have a ringing appeal. And there's that grand little comedy, "Dayspring Remembered," with all its merry charlatanry about Chaucer studies. There are also some bright travel books: I'd certainly like to have a complete edition of Kipling.

A few years ago, when I had the pleasure of meeting Dr. Shahane, who is Senior Professor of English at Osmania University, Hyderabad, India, and who has studied and taught in America (he has his Ph.D. from Leeds, in England), we discussed the possibility of his writing a book for this Crosscurrents/Modern Critiques series. We talked about E. M. Forster, about whom each of us has written, and whom Dr. Shahane knew (I had the pleasure of some correspondence with Forster and of meeting him once; I had written a little book about him); Dr. Shahane would have liked to give us a book on Forster, but that author was already dealt with excellently in our series by Norman Kelvin. I suggested that Dr. Shahane write a book on Kipling for us, presenting the Indian point of view. The critical study which follows is the happy result.

There have been two books about Kipling from an Eastern prospect, one by an Indian (K. Bhaskara Rao) and one by a Pakistani (Sajjad Husain), both of them revisions of doctoral dissertations. Dr. Shahane, in preparing this original study, worked among the Kipling material in the Berg Collection at the New York Public Library and at the British

Museum. He went to Bombay to visit Kipling's birthplace, and for further consideration of sites connected with Kipling, also visited Punjab and Kashmir. Above all he has written a book that is stimulating and informative.

His subtitle, Activist and Artist, suggests one of the major trends of this volume, in which Kipling is viewed as an intellectual activist becoming an imaginative artist. The various aspects of his creative self are discussed with an admirable thoroughness, bringing to light various matters that only a native of India, deeply versed in English literature, could recognize and interpret. This applies especially to Dr. Shahane's lengthy treatment of Kim, which he discusses as a search for identity and as Kipling's finest achievement. Here and in other discoveries he makes in Kipling's writings, Dr. Shahane gives us a new perspective on the man and writer and, I think, makes an important contribution to present-day literary studies.

HARRY T. MOORE

Southern Illinois University
March 21, 1973

Acknowledgments

The author and publisher wish to express their thanks to Mrs. George Bambridge; Macmillan & Co. Ltd., London; Macmillan Company of Canada, Ltd.; Doubleday & Co., Inc.; and A. P. Watt & Son for permission to quote from Rudyard Kipling's writings.

The author wishes to express gratitude to his colleagues Mr. B. N. Joshi, Dr. Sivaram Krishna, and Mr. N. R. Sastri for their help and suggestions in the revising of the manuscript.

Also, the author wishes to record his thanks to the librarian of the New York Public Library, who allowed him to use the Berg collection and see the rare Kipling manuscripts and drawings. And thanks are also due to the librarian at Wayne State University Library for his assistance in obtaining critical material on Kipling.

Introduction

When Kipling criticism is extensive and voluminous, why a new book on Kipling? The answer to this pertinent question is provided in the title of the book, *Rudyard Kipling: Activist and Artist*. The aim of the study is to explore the vital relationship between activism and art in Kipling's total achievement.

Since there are too many general commentaries on Kipling's life and work, this study aims at detailed textual analyses and explication and therefore has to be selective in view of the large corpus of Kipling's creative work. However, one introductory chapter outlining the main events in the author's life and relating them to his art is written as a setting to present his philosophy of life in terms of the main thesis of activism, and its transformation into art.

Kim, Kipling's masterpiece, has been explicated in detail and an entire chapter is devoted to it. The stories, the poems, and *Kim* have been interpreted from the Indian point of view, which may be an innovation in Kipling criticism.

VASANT A. SHAHANE

Hyderabad, India.
February 10, 1973.

Mr. Kipling knows and appreciates the English in India, and is a born story-teller and a man of humour into the bargain. He is also singularly versatile, and equally at home in humour and pathos.[2]

Although, "the extreme shortness of the stories" was considered an advantage by the reviewer, he felt that "as they are read in a few minutes, their incidents are easily forgotten." He conceded, however, "that they may be read again with fresh pleasure after a short interval."

There was also a perceptive review of this book written by Andrew Lang. Although his brief note on *Departmental Ditties*, as already stated, was marked by critical naïveté and superficial understanding, his comprehensive review of *Plain Tales from the Hills* in the *Daily News* shows a greater awareness of Kipling's qualities: "Mr. Kipling's tales really are of an extraordinary charm and fascination, not to all readers no doubt, but certainly to many men. His is more a man's book than a woman's book."[3]

Another significant early estimate of Kipling's stature as a writer is that of Henry James. Describing him as "the star of the hour," and "an infant monster," James tried to give his impressions in a letter (October 30, 1891) to Robert Louis Stevenson:

That little black demon of a Kipling will perhaps have leaped upon your silver strand by the time this reaches you. He publicly left England to embrace you many weeks ago—carrying literary genius out of the country with him in his pocket.[4]

Although the tone of this letter is slightly ironical, a letter written to his brother William James is significant in that Henry James tried to differentiate Kipling's individuality as a creative writer, by drawing a distinction between intelligence and genius. On February 6, 1892 he wrote: "Kipling strikes me personally as the most complete man of genius (as distinct from fine intelligence) that I have ever known."[5]

Stevenson's reaction to Kipling was characteristically ambiguous. He had undoubted admiration for him and wrote to Henry James (though in a slightly mocking tone) that he considered Kipling as "by far the most promising young man who has appeared since-ahem-I appeared." [6] Probably Stevenson felt that he and James and the other writers of his generation had begun to be "old fogies" and, therefore, "it was high time *something* rose to take our places." He recognized that Kipling with his perspicacity and varied gifts had the necessary stature to occupy this place. But he was also aware of Kipling's "copiousness and haste" which tended to neutralize whatever creative talent he possessed. Stevenson, therefore, had serious reservations about Kiplng's real quality as a writer.

The same critical ambiguity is apparent in the article written by Humphrey Ward (1845–1926) in the *Times* (London). [7] He recognized that Kipling possessed undoubted faculties of keen observation and incisive writing. This was particularly evident, as Ward could easily see, in Kipling's knowledge of Indian life which would be extraordinary in any writer and phenomenal in one so young. Ward rightly felt that Kipling's tales of Indian life "tapped a new vein." "Mr. Kipling has the merit of having tapped a new vein and of having worked it out with real originality." But this was the limit to which Ward went in his critical estimate for, like other contemporary Kipling critics, he had his own reservations and wrote: "We are far from asserting that Mr. Kipling has yet made any claim to a place in the first rank of contemporary writers."

But it is curious that notwithstanding these reservations regarding Kipling's stature, there was a spontaneous appreciation of his work—particularly of his poetry—by many distinguished contemporaries. It is said, for instance, that on the publication of "Danny Deever," one of Kipling's early ballads, in the *Scots Observer* (February 1890), an ardent admirer, W. E. Henley, stood up and attempted to dance on his wooden legs. Similarly, Professor Masson, the serious-minded scholar of Milton, was so overwhelmed by the quality of Kipling's ballads that he waved a copy before his class and shouted with joy, "Here's Literature! Here's Literature at last! "

Kipling's literary reputation is thus full of curious anomalies. In spite of academic neglect and indifference he continued to be an extremely popular writer. The young read his *Jungle Books* with avidity and the old read and reread his stories for superb entertainment. He was rich and famous, by far the most quoted of contemporary writers, the most talked-about, the most sought after by snobs and sightseers.[8] As Charles Morgan, commenting on the various Kipling editions published by Macmillan in England, has pointed out:

> Year by year the wise men held their breath and wondered whether by now the public demand for old wine in new bottles was exhausted. The cautious feared it might be, but they were always wrong.[9]

The fact remains, however, that the academic critics overlooked Kipling's achievement and tended to regard him as outside the mainstream of British literary tradition. They assumed an air of mute, almost studied, indifference toward him and he rarely received the critical attention that is due to a front-rank writer. They regarded him, by and large, as a poet of barrack-rooms, a composer of ballads and comic tidbits, and a writer of amusing satirical verse which lacked philosophical or intellectual depth. Besides, for the popular mind, Kipling invariably represented as Robert Buchanan has put it as early as 1900, "the voice of the hooligan," [10] the cult of cruelty and violence. All this led to a denunciation as strange as it is anomalous since it coincided with his immense popularity. But, by 1941, as Edmund Wilson has pointed out, it was felt that Kipling was "written out." Max Beerbohm's well-known drawing of Kipling—"On the Shelf" —in the posture of a tarnished brass idol gathering dust, is a significant reflector of the time-spirit.

In the twenty-five years following the death of Rudyard Kipling (1936) the same situation continued, more or less unchanged, and not a single, sustained piece of criticism was written on him during this period. T. S. Eliot's well-known introduction [11] to his *Choice of Kipling's Verse* (1943), is, of course, an exception to the general denunciation of Kipling. Eliot drew attention to the need for a candid revaluation of the achievement of Kipling, whom he described as "the most inscrutable of authors." [12] But the echo of the familiar critical debunking could still be heard, as in H. E. Bates's assessment. In *The Modern Short Story* (1943) Bates categorically declared [13] Kipling to be an "execrable" poet who represents "a dying hierarchy, cruelty, violence and stupid complacency and reaction." Similarly, Rupert Croft-Cooke in his *Rudyard Kipling* (1948) examines his achievement in terms of the all too familiar theme of British imperialism and fails to take into account other vital factors. Thus the forties seems a negative period in the appreciation of Kipling's stature as a writer.

It is probable that this failure of criticism to come to terms with Kipling's achievement as a creative writer is rooted, partly, in the enigmatic personality of the man himself. There is undoubtedly an integral link between his personal life and his creative work but many of the vital details have been so far unavailable. However, the few perceptive insights into his character which we do possess now reveal him to be a rather complex personality difficult to be explained away by any of the facile generalizations with which he is usually dismissed in critical discussions. The all-too-familiar view of Kipling as an imperialist or a jingoist or an adolescent, though gifted, writer, or a poet of action and heroism who thrived on portraying cruelty, brutality, and violence seems today, in retrospect, a case of rather misguided, drastic oversimplification.

One of the difficulties, therefore, in the assessment of Kipling's real achievement is the absence of a genuinely revealing and authentic biography of this complex figure. His biographers, so far, though competent and sincere, do not seem to have transcended Victorian discreetness and Edwardian punctiliousness in analyzing this puzzling phenomenon in English literature. Hilton Brown's biography, *Rudyard Kipling: A New Appreciation* (1945), does succeed in bringing out something of the complexity of Kipling, yet it is rather apologetic in tone and sketchy in treatment. Similarly, Charles E. Carrington's *Rudyard Kipling: His Life and Work* (1955) is comprehensive, scholarly, and painstakingly written; yet it smacks of the formal strain of an official biography. A new biography of Rudyard Kipling based on new materials such as his letters and the unpublished writing and sketches may prove a boon to Kipling scholars. This biography must be marked by empathy as well as detachment, an intense admiration for Kipling's remarkable qualities as well as the frank portrayal of his weaknesses. A candid and objective life of Rudyard Kipling is still to be written. If and when it appears, one can presume with reasonable certainty that it will offer significant biographical data, particularly of Kipling's childhood and adolescence, which will be very pertinent to an understanding of the theme of violence in his early work. It is impossible to disentangle the otherwise baffling cult of cruelty in his stories. Thus a refreshingly new link may be forged between his life and his work.

The intimate connection between Kipling's life and creative work becomes particularly meaningful in the context of the quest for identity and the desire for the realization of selfhood which are evident in Anglo-Indian writing. Kipling's sense of identity, as Thomas N. Cross [14] has pointed out, is rooted in his personal life and its problems. The basic problem is whether Kipling had a sense of belonging to the world in which he found himself, and a deep sense of involvement with it. But this major issue subsumes a number of related problems: whether Kipling had, especially in his childhood and adolescence, a stable and steady social and individual life with normal responses within and without his family and immediate society. This can only be examined in the light of the events and experiences of Kipling's life.

Rudyard Kipling was born in Bombay on December 30, 1865. His father, John Lockwood Kipling, Professor of Architectural Sculpture at the Bombay School of Art, had arrived in Bombay with his wife, Alice, in May of that year. Alice Macdonald was one of five pretty daughters of a Wesleyan minister. She belonged to a distinguished family: her sister Georgiana, married Edward Burne-Jones; another sister, Agnes, became the wife of Edward Poynter; the third sister, Louisa, became the mother of Stanley Baldwin, the famous statesman and Britain's Prime Minister. It is obvious that Rudyard Kipling was well connected and he had close associations with members of the Pre-Raphaelite brotherhood.

John Lockwood Kipling and Alice settled down in the small, well-knit British community in the city of Bombay. Mrs. Kipling had a painful and prolonged labor before Rudyard was born on December 30. Rudyard was told that he arrived into this world safely because one of the servants had actually offered to sacrifice a kid to the Hindu goddess, *Kali*, in return for his safe birth. Rudyard's childhood was spent in the lovely city of Bombay, in the large, spacious rooms and the garden of his father's home. As a child he observed the beauty of the sea and the lovely colors of the sky. His mother wrote, when he was only six months old, that the boy "notices everything that he sees" and that he was deeply attached to his *ayah*, the Indian nurse. An Indian woman of Goan origin, Rudyard's nurse was an extremely devoted and sincere maid. She was a Roman Catholic and knew Hindi and Marathi. It seems to me that this *ayah* and the Hindu servant Meeta, exercised a much deeper influence on the child than his own parents. The story "Baa, Baa, Black Sheep," which begins with a portrayal of the affectionate relationship between Punch (Ruddy) and the *ayah* and Meeta, is clearly autobiographical in character: "They were putting Punch to bed—the *ayah* and the *hamal* and Meeta, the big *Surti* boy with the red and gold turban. Judy, already tucked inside her mosquito-curtains, was nearly asleep."

> "Punch-*baba* going to bye-lo?" said the *ayah*, suggestively. "No," said Punch. "Punch-*baba* wants the story about the Ranee that was turned into a tiger. Meeta must tell it, and the *hamal* shall hide behind the door and make tiger-noises at the proper time." [15]

Meeta began to relate the story and Punch shouted with joy: " 'Top!" Punch wanted a *put-put* (a bicycle), but he was told by the nurse that he was soon to leave and that "there will be no Punch-*baba* to pull my hair any more." The nurse sighed softly, for "the boy of the household was very dear to her heart." Punch asked them whether he was to go to "Nassick [a city with a cool climate about 150 miles from Bombay] where the Ranee-Tiger lives." Meeta, the man-servant, told Punch that the boy might be leaving for *Belait* (Britain). "Will you take Meeta with you to *Belait*?" "You shall all come," said Punch, from the height of Meeta's strong arms. "Meeta and the *ayah* and the *hamal* and Bhini-in-the-Garden, and the salaam-Captain-Sahib-snake-man." This has an obvious reference to Rudyard's servants, the *ayah* and Meeta who nourished his imagination on the myths and legends of India. Moreover, it is interesting to note that both Rudyard and Trix, his younger sister, learnt to speak in Hindi first and only later in English. The servants, it is said, dressed them for dinner and as they were about to enter the dining room, prompted them "to speak English now to Papa and Mama." (One can, of course, trace Kim's extraordinary facility in Hindustani to Rudyard's early ac-quaintance with the language.) This question of language and early exposure to Indian folktales and myths has a peculiar bearing on Kipling's quest for identity, on his search for a stabilizing center, a core of being with which he could identify himself. The apparently alienating influence of a foreign language on Kipling's mind is a fact which probably complicated this search for identity.

There are other aspects of Kipling's childhood experiences in India and England which have clear relevance to the choice and formulation of his themes. Near Lockwood, Kipling's home in Bombay, was a Parsee Tower of Silence, a kind of a deep, dry well in which were hung the corpses of the people of the Parsee community. This was the usual Parsee ritual in regard to the dead. Vultures would gather and eat away the flesh, and on one occasion the putrid arm of a child was noticed in the Kiplings' garden. Ruddy's curiosity was aroused by this strange object but his mother forbade him from asking any questions or discussing the matter further. But Ruddy already knew the truth from his *ayah*. This was probably his earliest encounter with the fact of death. The sight of the flesh of the dead must have given him feelings of revulsion, and the themes of human cruelty and violence in his work can possibly be linked with these events in his early life—though the problem is far more complex than such a facile connection would warrant.

Ruddy made his first voyage to England when in 1868 Mrs. Kipling left for home for her confinement. England to him seemed dark, dismal, and cold compared with the sunny warmth of Bombay. He also felt the difference between his warmhearted and affectionate *ayah* of his Bombay home and the efficient but indifferent and cold servants in England. Mrs. Kipling gave birth to Trix, and they returned to India in autumn and resumed their happy routine.

In April 1871 the Kiplings left for England again taking Ruddy and Trix with them. Then in December 1871 they left the children in the care of a Mrs. Holloway at Southsea in England and returned to India. Trix and Ruddy couldn't really understand why their parents left them to the care of the Holloways and why they didn't even say good-bye before leaving for Bombay. Trix wrote later that "the real tragedy" of their early life was their "inability to understand why our parents had deserted us. We had had no preparation or explanation, it was like a double death, or rather, like an avalanche that had swept away everything happy and familiar."

The reason lies, partly, in Rudyard's mother, who was a self-willed and assertive woman. She was highly impulsive, and sometimes sulked and at other times revolted against the obtrusive pieties of a rigid mid-Victorian family. She was often scolded by her parents for returning home too late at night, and was even accused of being a flirt. In her anger she once threw a lock of John Wesley's hair into the fire. She was, however, quick of wit, jovial, and highly individualistic. She had broken at least three engagements before marrying John Lockwood Kipling.

On her second visit to England after marriage, Alice saw the gradual break up of the Macdonald family. Her two sisters, Agnes and Louisa, subsequent to their marriage, had left home, and her father had become an invalid. Therefore, Ruddy was left for sometime with Louisa Baldwin, and he proved to be a difficult boy in the Baldwin household.

Ruddy, who was always pampered by his Indian *ayah* at his home in Bombay, proved to be too demanding in the sedate Baldwin household in England. "He turned the house into a bear-garden." Even the old Mrs. Macdonald, Alice's mother, heaved a sigh of relief on her daughter's departure from her home. The mother had on occasion exchanged sharp words with Alice, and neither could get over it. It was this rather delicate and tense experience which made Alice reject the offer of the Baldwins to have the two children stay with them. This made Alice decide to leave Ruddy and Trix in the care of a Mrs. Holloway at Horne Lodge in December 1871.

There can be little doubt that Rudyard's stay with the Holloways was crucial in several respects. It not only brought him into contact with a set of intolerant people for almost the first time, it also exposed him to what can be described as deliberate, motiveless violence and cruelty. Rudyard himself describes his experiences at Horne Lodge (in *Something of Myself*) with restraint, but with utmost candor. The Holloway home is described as "the House of Desolation," [16] a place of deep mental and physical suffering, loneliness, isolation, and humiliation. "The cult of violence" with which most critics identify Kipling—and unjustly dismiss him—originated probably from this early encounter with cruelty.

Mrs. Holloway was a heartless, cruel, unsympathetic, rigid woman, whereas her husband, Mr. Holloway, a retired naval officer, was a kindhearted man. However, he died a few months after the children's arrival. They, therefore, were left at the mercy of Mrs. Holloway and her narrow-minded, hostile son, Harry. Harry looked down upon Ruddy's Anglo-Indian background and made fun of him in every possible way. Mrs. Holloway, affected as she was by her narrow, religious outlook, took serious exception to Ruddy's easygoing manner. Once Ruddy was severely reprimanded for just smiling on his way back from church, and he was punished because he could not give any reasonable cause for his smile. He was branded as a liar. Mrs. Holloway often beat him to drive home her puritanical rigor and disciplinary rigidity. Ruddy was so frightened of her frequent beatings that once for fear of punishment he didn't show her his school report and threw it away. He was soon found out, beaten, and made to walk the street to the school in Southsea with a card tagged on his jacket bearing the word *liar* in capital letters. Mrs. Holloway probably had a "vivid" but diseased imagination. She tried to present a grim picture of Christian Hell to Ruddy to overawe him. In this Hell, she told him, liars were punished severely by being tied to the wheels of fire. She also pictured to him the rewards of the good life, the Christian Heaven.

Harry, similarly, took pleasure in torturing Ruddy. When the boy began to lose his normal sight, due to excessive reading, Mrs. Holloway tried to adduce this as an additional evidence of his hypocrisy. But this affliction proved to be a liberating factor and he was taken away from the Holloways in March 1877.

Rudyard began wearing glasses and was enrolled at a boarding school, "Westward Ho!" on January 16, 1878. This preparatory, public school was primarily run for students seeking an army career and was administered by retired army personnel. But the headmaster, Cormell Price, was an old and trusted friend of John Lockwood Kipling and he took great interest in Ruddy's upbringing and educational career. Moreover, Cormell and Burne-Jones were college-mates at Oxford. Ruddy was physically not quite strong and his weak eyesight prevented him from participating in the sports of the school. In 1881, therefore, Cormell Price gave him the editorship of the school journal, the *United Services College Chronicle*, and this opportunity in his early life paved the way for Kipling's journalistic and literary career. He left "Westward Ho!" in July 1882. During the four and a half years Rudyard wrote several poems, essays, and schoolboy skits. One poem "Ave Imperatix," which appeared in the eighth number of the *Chronicle* (March 20, 1882), is especially suggestive of the time-spirit as well as the tendencies of the young Kipling.

Such greeting as should come from those
Whose fathers faced the Sepoy hordes,

Or served You in the Russian snows,
    And, dying, left their sons their swords.

And some of us have fought for You
    Already in the Afghan Pass
Or where the scarce-seen smoke-puffs flew
    From Boer marksmen in the grass;

And all are bred to do Your will
    By land and sea—wherever flies
The Flag, to fight and follow still
    And work Your Empire's destinies.

The third stanza, as H. L. Varley has pointed out, shows that Kipling as a young man "is very committed to strong national patriotism of the 'my country, right or wrong' variety." [17]

It was Kipling's mother who got his first book, *School Boy Lyrics* (1881), printed, which included his poems published in the *United Services College Chronicle* and in the family journal, *The Scribbler*, which he produced in 1879 with the help and cooperation of his cousins. In school, Rudyard came under the influence of his teacher, Mr. Crofts, who inspired him to read classics, Shakespeare, and great English novels. The young Kipling was particularly fond of Fielding, Smollett, Dickens, and Thackeray. He was deeply influenced by the poetry of Robert Browning and the works of Emerson, Carlyle, and Ruskin. These early readings molded Kipling's outlook on life. In 1884 he and his sister Beatrice published *Echoes*, which contained thirty-nine poems, thirty-two written by him and the rest by his sister. There were parodies of Tennyson, Browning, Swinburne, and of various nursery rhymes.

Kipling, after his return to India in 1882, began his journalistic career at the age of seventeen at Lahore, on the staff of the *Civil and Military Gazette*. The usual practice of British-owned Indian newspapers was to recruit young and promising Englishmen and train them in the journalistic skills. They were initiated into the various departments and later promoted to "subbing" or subeditorship. The pale

Rudyard entered the offices of the *Gazette* with his "cheery voice and eager manner, a perpetual habit of wiping his glasses clear of perspiration."

There are many claimants, however, to the privileged position of Kipling's sponsorship in journalism. J. P. Collins declares [18] that it was the late Sir George Allen, the chief of *Pioneer* at Allahabad and a friend of Lockwood Kipling, who suggested this assignment since Ruddy was fit neither for a military career nor could he attend, for financial reasons, Oxford or Cambridge. It is said that Sir David Masson, the proprietor of the *Pioneer*, took the initiative in launching young Ruddy on his career. Also, that Sir William Rattigan, the eminent lawyer and judge, had had a hand in guiding Kipling's journalistic art. The name of the well-known philanthropist, Sir James Walker, is also associated with Kipling's early fortunes.

The *Civil and Military Gazette* aimed at developing a pattern characteristic of the prestigious *Pall Mall Gazette* of London. It afforded great scope for Rudyard to write crisp sketches, stories, and verses. He worked under Stephen Wheeler, the chief editor of the *Gazette*. Half the staff consisted of Englishmen who were jealous of Rudyard because he was given very responsible and important assignments by Wheeler. The other half were Indians who were on cordial terms with Rudyard. He quickly learnt all the routine work of reporting, editing, and feature writing. He worked very hard, at least eight hours a day in the unbearable heat of Lahore, and persevered in his duties in spite of attacks of fever and other tropical diseases. He wrote stories, verses, dramatic pieces, satirical skits, and lively descriptions of the Indian scene. He also covered important public events and reported them in a racy style. In 1884 he was deputed to Patiala State in the Punjab to cover Lord Ripon's visit to the capital. In 1885 he wrote an impressive report of the reception given to the viceroy at Rawalpindi by Amir Abdul Rahman of the North-West Frontier Province. He visited Kashmir, met the Maharajah and later wrote an excellent account of his coronation in Srinagar. He often visited Simla, the summer capital of the Government of India, where he got all the official gossip and covered it skillfully in his columns. Kipling was an honest, conscientious, competent journalist who spared no pains to achieve a high standard of journalistic reporting and commentary.

It was during the early period of his journalistic career that Kipling wrote the famous *Departmental Ditties* (1886). The book appeared to be almost a government publication; its format resembled a large official envelope and it was tied in the middle with a red tape. It proved very popular and ran into seven editions by 1892. Its satirical assault was directed against ignorance and knavery. Kipling's satire was aimed at those British members of the services who thrived on bribery and corruption and also those at home in England who took an uncharitable view of the sincere, hardworking, devoted members of the British civil and armed services in India. These Englishmen, Kipling suggests, are too ignorant to have any realistic sense or understanding of the complexities and uncertainties of the challenging tasks of the services in India. They lead a sheltered life in their cosy homes in England and have little or no notion of the difficulties of living in a tropical country. As editor of the *Gazette* Kipling supported the official position on the Ilbert Act of 1884, which permitted the native Indian judges to try the whites. His press had a large stake in governmental policies since it was patronized by the Punjab Government in many ways. On the evening his published defense of the Act appeared in the *Gazette*, Kipling visited the Anglo-Indian Club and was almost hissed by a number of irritated Anglo-Indian women for his support of the Ilbert Act.[19] He pooh-poohed their silly objections and was not much taken in by the narrowness and arrogance of the ruling English class in India. Criticizing the ignorance of the majority of the British regarding service conditions in India, he wrote:

> Sing a song of six pence
>   Purchased by our lives
> Decent English gentlemen
>   Roasting with their wives,
> In the plains of India

> *Where like flies they die.*
> *Isn't that a wholesome risk*
> *To get our living by?* [20]

Thus Kipling's attitude toward the British—his imperialistic stance—is far too complicated to be explained away by a few glib generalizations.

H. L. Varley has pointed out that "Ignorance in England and knavery in India are the two fundamental points of satire, not only in the poetry but also in the collections of short stories" of Kipling in this early phase. The young Rudyard's captivating stories, *The Phantom 'Rickshaw* (1888), *Wee Willie Winkie* (1888), *Under the Deodars* (1888), *In Black and White* (1888), amply illustrate this satirical trend in relation to Anglo-India. His well-known *Plain Tales from the Hills* and *Soldiers Three* also appeared in 1888. At this time Rudyard left Lahore for Allahabad to edit the *Pioneer*, which enlarged the area for his exploration of the Anglo-Indian scene. The creative and journalistic work of Kipling in this early phase has not yet been fully and accurately ascertained and assessed, partly because he wrote a great deal of it anonymously. Moreover, he used about twenty-five pseudonyms such as R. K., K. R. Nickson, Rudy, Yussuf, etc., even in his special write-ups, making identification difficult. This peculiar anonymity or assumption of multiple personality becomes meaningful in the context of his search for true identity.

The assumption of the multiple personality of Kipling is curiously suggested by the "Original pen-and-ink sketches and caricatures" which he himself had drawn. These sketches are preserved in a small-book form consisting of twelve pages in the Berg Collection of rare manuscripts in the New York Public Library (Holograph No. 464 and A 657). Kipling in these self-drawn sketches seems to be a perplexed person who is dressed as a gentleman. Each sketch has a peculiarity of it own. There are drawings of animals, too, of horse, deer, and monkey. Kipling's various sketches show an aspect of his multiple personality and also his quest for what he really was, his true identity.

Even in this early stage of Kipling's journalistic and literary career, he had developed his distinctive style as well as his minor eccentricities. A columnist in New Delhi's *Statesman*, commenting on what he calls the eccentricities of Rudyard's genius, says:

> In his chambers he had a huge roll-top desk at which he did his work. . . . He also had a Gurkha "Kukri" [a sharp implement], a particularly fine one with a razor edge. With this he carved on his desk in letters at least six inches high, "Oft was I weary when I sat at thee." When he was thinking out details for a story, he would sit in a chair and chop at the sides with the "Kukri," reducing the furniture to mere fragments. He was always unconscious of his actions when composing.[21]

As a journalist, Kipling was a keen observer. He tried to get news from varied sources, writes an Indian lecturer in Journalism, M. R. Dua, "from courts, ball rooms, clubs, soldiers' mess. His copy always had the tone of a smoking-room conversation." [22] The apparent abruptness and casualness of Kipling's early writing may thus be traced to the original sources of his inspiration, the soldier's rough talk or a beggar's tale, which he tried to turn into enduring artistic stories.

Toward the close of his journalistic career in India Rudyard Kipling was recalled from Allahabad to Lahore (1889) to work as assistant editor of the *Civil and Military Gazette*, since its editor, Kay Robinson, was taken ill. In 1889 Kipling, however, left India for England and settled down in London. Here he came into close contact with W. E. Henley, the editor of the *Scots Observer*, in which his early verse and *Barrack-Room Ballads* were published.

In the early phase of his journalistic career Rudyard owed a great deal to the chief editor of the *Gazette*, Stephen Wheeler, who was a man of wide scholarship and perceptive understanding. Wheeler was always forceful in his write-ups, and he knew Persian, Urdu, and Hindi. He was a close personal friend of the Kipling family and had great respect for John Lockwood Kipling's knowledge of Indian antiquity and Alice's sparkling wit. Although he refused to write a

book of personal memoirs on Rudyard Kipling, he had many
anecdotes and personal experiences of the Kiplings to tell in
lively company. He confirmed Rudyard's view of his mother
as "the wittiest woman in India." One of his anecdotes told
of a grand reception at the governor's house where the host,
His Excellency, seemed engaged in a long chat with Alice
punctuated by ripples of laughter, while the other fashionable
ladies of Lahore looked on with envy. "You've monopolised
His Excellency a nice long time," said one of them bitterly
when the spell was over. Her light retort was a whispered
"Oh, my dear, if only you'd heard—it wasn't the length but
the breadth—of it." [23]

During his stay at Allahabad (1887–89) Rudyard Kipling
met Professor S. A. Hill and his wife "Ted." Rudyard and
Ted (nine years older than Kipling) developed a romantic
relationship, "a puppy love," and she became his confidant,[24]
though only for a short time. The Hills and Rudyard traveled
together from India to the United States via Japan and
Canada in 1889. In the United States Rudyard met Caroline
Hill, the younger sister of Ted, and this event led to another
short-lived romance. On his return to London in the winter
of 1889, Kipling met Wolcott Balestier, an American who
was an American publisher's representative, through Edmund Gosse, and this turned out to be one of the most
intimate of all personal relationships in Kipling's life. Kipling and Wolcott Balestier had a brief spell of literary col-
laboration in writing *The Naulahka, A Story of West and
East* (1897). Kipling began to suffer from ill health and
undertook a long voyage to Africa, Cape of Good Hope,
Ceylon, and India. In Bombay he heard the sad news of
Wolcott's death. He immediately returned to his home in
London and married Caroline, Wolcott's sister, in January
1892. "Kipling and Carrie," writes Thomas N. Cross, "now
positively dashed into marriage, with a special licence, in
eight days with five people in the congregation." [25] Kipling's
relationship with Wolcott and Carrie requires a deeper understanding and a closer analysis than what has so far been
made. This is clearly an area of interesting exploration for
the future biographer of Kipling.

Rudyard and Caroline undertook a voyage, as part of their honeymoon, to the East, but at Yokohama they learnt of the sudden failure of their bank, and they had to proceed to the United States almost penniless. The Kiplings arrived at Caroline's family home in Brattleboro, Vermont, and stayed at a small house known as "Bliss Cottage." Here in 1892 their first child, Josephine, was born. Soon after, Kipling's books began to sell well, and out of the sizable royalties he built a spacious house and named it "Naulakha." The Kiplings lived in Naulakha for about four years, visiting Bermuda and Wiltshire on their holidays.

Kipling's American experience, if not quite exasperating, was not very exhilarating either. He was attracted by pretty and well-to-do American women, but he distrusted what Howard C. Rice has termed "Yankee curiosity," [26] though this was nothing more than the friendliness and get-together-ness of affectionate Americans. American reporters misinterpreted his casual remarks, especially in respect to a contemporary political problem over the boundary of Venezuela where Great Britain and the United States joined issues, and this political coloring showed Kipling in a very different light. Some Americans believed that Kipling remained a true Englishman at heart and that his patriotism was only sharpened by his long stay away from his home country. He therefore could not appreciate the idealistic gleam or pragmatic wisdom behind America's astounding success in industry and commerce. Although helped by his wife, he could not make substantial progress in adapting himself to American ways, and his peculiar patriotic feeling was unduly stirred by an occasional reference to "our hereditary foes." Nevertheless, he might have indeed settled down at Naulakha in Vermont had not the dispute over a small piece of land with his brother-in-law, Beatty, assumed serious proportions. In fact the quarrel between brother and sister started at dinner in Beatty's house, and Beatty said to the Kiplings: "You're in my house; you're my guest but by Christ, once you've left it, I'll never speak to you again as long as I live." [27] The matter was taken to court, Kipling testified to Beatty's threats of physical violence. Although Beatty was held in four hundred dollars bail by the grand jury, the trial did grave damage to Kipling. The American press parodied Kipling's plight ("Rudyard, running for his life" in the *Reformer*) and Kipling left Vermont in August (1897), before the meeting of the grand jury which was scheduled for September, never to return. Yet the Kiplings visited New York in February 1899 (their last visit); Rudyard was taken ill during this visit and their eldest child, Josephine, died in New York at this time.

Kipling had had many pleasant experiences in Vermont. One cannot overlook the fact that during this Vermont period he produced some of his best work, including *Kim*. It will be unwise to make any fuss over Rudyard's family quarrel with Beatty or his casual remarks on American life or political events. For, it was in Vermont that Kipling blossomed into a creative genius. He created a brave new world of Mougli and Rikki-Tikki, and *Kim*, his supreme achievement, emerged from the Vermont phase of his literary career. Therefore, the Kipling that quarreled with Beatty will be rightly forgotten and the Kipling that rose in splendor over the romantic and esoteric world of *Kim* will be ever remembered.

Another important phase of Kipling's literary career is associated with his stay in South Africa at Wash (1899). He formed a deep friendship with Cecil Rhodes, who offered him a house on his estate. This house, "The Woolsack," became Kipling's home from 1900 to 1908. Yet Kipling never experienced a genuine sense of belonging to any particular country for all time. Even in England he felt deeply alienated from common folk. Still, he was fascinated by English history and the remarkable achievement of the British in the nineteenth century. While he was in England, he was homesick for America, South Africa, and India. He had developed a very deep sense of attachment to India. "There are only two places in the world where I want to live," he declared, "Bombay and Brattleboro. And I can't live in either one."

During the last two decades of his life, Kipling suffered from ill health and a steep decline in popularity. His only son, John, was killed in the war (1916), and his body was never found. This tragic loss inspired Kipling to write an arresting account of *The Irish Guards in the Great War*. This irreparable loss and an operation performed in 1926 saddened his later life. He died in London on January 18, 1936. The burial took place with pomp in the poet's corner in Westminster Abbey on January 23, 1936. By a curious coincidence Kipling lies buried near T. S. Eliot in the Abbey. By another equally curious coincidence the body of an Indian leader, Shahpurji Sakalatwala,[28] was cremated on the day of Kipling's burial. Later the Indian mourners of Sakalatwala joined those of Kipling. Thus, even in his moment of death a strange link seems to have been established between Kipling and India.

Kipling, the first man in England to be so honored, was awarded the Nobel Prize for literature in 1907 at the age of forty-two. This was a magnificient international recognition of his multifaceted genius and his remarkable achievement. His greatness essentially springs from his activism, his belief in the discipline of organized work which finds creative expression in his art. He brings strength and vitality to the anemic world of late nineteenth-century England, the little literary world of Oscar Wilde and Beardsley. He also created a "mystique" of the Empire. Kipling is intellectually an activist, but in the process of realizing his self, he is transformed into an artist.

2

Alienated Activist and Imperialist

The late-Victorian adulation of Kipling as an inexplicable literary miracle and the post–World War denunciation of him as an inveterate imperialist are both extreme attitudes in evaluating his complexity. These divergent critical perspectives drastically reduce the nature and quality of Kipling's achievement to highly simplistic categories. Consequently, the central reality of Kipling's cosmos, in which contraries such as the real and the ideal, the physical and the spiritual, the cruel and the compassionate are harmonized into art, is overlooked.

The core of Kipling's complexity as an artist lies in his alienated activism. As E. San Juan, Jr. has perceptively pointed out,[1] Kipling is essentially a spokesman of activism which is a significant strand of Victorian thought. In its simple form "activism" may be described as "the doctrine or policy of being active or doing things with energy and decision." It postulates a life of vigorous, dynamic action committed to the belief in man's ability to transform society through this action. Though activism as a doctrine can be traced to the adventurous spirit of the Victorian age, it was also embodied, earlier, in the Faustian motif of the endless quest for experience and action. In this regard, the spirit of Faust, immortalized by Goethe, is symbolic of the growth of European civilization with its irrepressible longing for action, adventure, and knowledge.

In the Victorian age, this longing to extend the boundaries of knowledge and experience ceased to be merely an intellectual doctrine and became a plank for action. Progress was no longer an inner, spiritual growth but an external, tangible manifestation. The phenomenal growth of science and technology in this period was only an activistic extension of a fundamental belief in man's endless capacity for meaningful action. The Great Exhibition of 1851, held at South Kensington, featured as "Britain Can Make It" Exposition, was a symbol not only of Britain's significant achievement in industry and commerce but also of the activistic creed which formed an essential component of Victorian thought. This remarkable achievement in the world of trade and commerce coincided, significantly enough, with England's expanding political power as an enlightened colonizer. This was, in fact, the outcome of the enterprising, dynamic spirit of its great and adventurous pioneers. Thus, activistic creed was a major assumption behind England's men of destiny, behind the architects of the vast citadels and ramparts of the British Empire.

Since activism is a positivistic doctrine, it is obvious that it should believe in the possibility of progressive perfection. One of the corollaries of the activistic creed is the concept of progress. This concept is especially associated, in the Victorian age, with Herbert Spencer (1820–1903). As a distinguished representative of contemporary philosophic thought, Spencer postulated the basic idea of force or energy which is, in his view, the true source of evolutionary process and development. Energy, for Spencer, is the ultimate principle in the cosmic design, and out of this inexhaustible energy springs the endless progress of humanity. This concept of energy and its meaningful application in the spheres of material and social life becomes the genesis of activism as a major strand of Victorian thought.

Although the philosophic dimension of the activistic doctrine was formulated by Spencer, its most gifted spokesman in contemporary literature was the poet laureate, Alfred Tennyson. Activism finds its most pervasive expression in his poem "Ulysses." Consumed by endless longing to traverse the entire universe, Ulysses "cannot rest from travel" and he becomes a symbol of the inveterate pilgrim "always roaming with a hungry heart." He ardently desires "to follow knowledge like a sinking star,/Beyond the utmost bound of human thought." He knows that death is the inevitable end, yet before this final event, he wishes to perform "some work of noble note." In a revealing moment of self-awareness, he articulates the tone and temper of the entire age:

> One equal temper of heroic hearts
> Made weak by time and fate, but strong in will
> To strive, to seek, to find, and not to yield.

In Ulysses's realization of this "temper of heroic hearts" an important activistic facet of Victorian thinking and feeling is effectively expressed. Similarly, in "Locksley Hall," Tennyson "dipt into the future," visualizing the great achievement of the "Parliament of Man, the Federation of the World." Thus the Tennysonian expression of Victorian activism is vitally linked with the enduring vision of man's progress in this world.

This prophetic fervor which characterized Tennyson found its clearest exponent in Thomas Carlyle, the distinguished littérateur of mid-Victorian England. Though Carlyle was primarily a transcendentalist and a mystic whose world view was based on the postulate of self-renunciation, he reinforced in his writings the basic premises of activism. For him work was worship and he exhorted his countrymen to follow the doctrines of duty and devoted work. Like Kipling, he underscored the imperative necessity to submit to Law and Duty and declared "Love not pleasure, love God." "This is the *Everlasting Yea*, wherein all contradiction is solved: wherein whoso walks and works, it is well with him." [2] In brief, to Carlyle work is Reality striving against Unreality. In the absence of meaningful endeavor, the world will become "a dark, wasteful chaos," while fruitful, purposive action will make it "a blooming, fertile, heaven-compassioned world." As a prophet of Victorian activism, Carlyle exhorted:

> Produce! Produce! Were it but the pitifullest infinitesimal fraction of a Product, produce it, in God's name! 'Tis the utmost thou hast in thee: out with it, then. Up, up!

Whatsoever thy hand findeth to do, do it with thy whole might. Work while it is called Today; for the Night cometh, wherein no man can work.[3]

In accordance with this, Carlyle praises work and workmen for their contribution to the task of nation building. "Venerable to me is the hard hand," he says, which is as "royal as the Sceptre of this Planet." [4] In his *Past and Present*, he pays glowing tributes to those who work with their hands for "there is a perennial nobleness, and even sacredness, in work." All doubt and scepticism, in fact, can be transcended through action alone.

The latest Gospel in this world is, Know thy work and do it. "Know thyself": long enough has that poor "self" of thine tormented thee; thou wilt never get to "know" it, I believe! Think it not thy business, this of knowing thyself; thou art an unknowable individual: know what thou canst work at; and work at it, like a Hercules! That will be thy better plan.[5]

Thus Victorian thought is deeply imbued with moral seriousness emerging from the cardinal principle of activism. This was the core of a consistently formulated and widely accepted philosophy of life.

The Victorian age, however, was marked by many diverse trends and conflicting beliefs, which were instituted as modes to achieve some sort of equilibrium. Activism, with its faith in energetic action, is one of these unifying or stabilizing forces. The peculiar fascination of activism was rooted in the fact that it linked itself to the primal urge for meaningful action which is imbedded in Western consciousness. In fact activism, as formulated by Rudolf Eucken (1846–1926), may be described as "a philosophy of creative will." The dynamic nature of the creative will in the activistic doctrine makes it peculiarly fascinating to the Western psyche. But in the Victorian milieu divergent tendencies continue to operate as undercurrents and therefore it is difficult to analyze and assess this age in terms of homogeneous systems of values. From this point of view, even Kipling's imperialism, which is only one facet of the activism of the age, is a product of many conflicting tendencies. It is necessary, therefore, to realize the limitations as well as the wider implications which inevitably operate in the working of the activistic doctrine.

A cardinal tenet of Victorian activism was its belief that the doctrine of action has its sanction in divine power. From this point of view, human energy and material success are only tangible shapes and forms of divine power and spiritual triumph. It is out of this assumption that Kipling's attempt to project a fusion of the finite and the infinite, the secular and the religious, the political and the moral, arises. In his poem "Recessional" Kipling makes a plea to Lord God to bless man's activistic efforts and to be with him always.

> If, drunk with sight of power, we loose
> 　Wild tongues that have not Thee in awe—
> Such boastings as the Gentiles use,
> 　Or lesser breeds without the Law—
> Lord God of Hosts, be with us yet,
> 　Lest we forget—lest we forget![6]

Kipling's plea to the Lord God of Hosts is obviously the expression of his faith in the close connection between divinity and the activist ideal.

Kipling's attempt to fuse into a totality the religious and the temporal aspects of life gives us a clue not only to his conception of law but also to his formulation of the imperialist ideal. His concept of law operates on many levels and it subsumes the biblical law or the moral law to which the interest of individuals must be subordinated in order to attain a high level of collective achievement. Thus it becomes not only the law of the community but also the higher law that governs society's moral ideals. In the former sense law is, in Lord Moulton's words, "the crystallized common-sense of the community," while in the latter sense it is, in Richard Hooker's words, "the voice of right reason." For Kipling the essential quality of law is the enrichment of human welfare in all aspects. In this regard he would agree with Dr. Johnson's conception of law as "the last result of human wisdom acting upon human experience for the benefit of the public."

It is against this background that one has to understand and assess Kipling's appreciation of the silent but significant role played by the civil service and the army in maintaining the British Empire. In Kipling's view the civil service, the army, and police are assigned the task of judicious and balanced implementation of the secular law of the community. Kipling is all praise for these people who maintain community life in a state of order and balance. But he is always aware of their suffering and alienation. In his poem "Gentlemen-Rankers" Kipling articulates the inwardly felt suffering of these devoted men.

We have done with Hope and Honour, we are lost to Love
     and Truth,
  We are dropping down the ladder rung by rung,
And the measure of our torment is the measure of our youth.[7]

Kipling identifies himself with these gentlemen-rankers, and several of his poems concerning the civil service and military personnel in India are marked by the pain of isolation and alienation from the native soil. "The Gentlemen-Rankers" open out their anguished hearts:

> *We're poor little lambs who've lost our way,*
> *Baa! Baa! Baa!*
> *We're little black sheep who've gone astray,*
> *Baa—aa—aa!*
> *Gentlemen-rankers out on the spree,*
> *Damned from here to Eternity,*
> *God ha' mercy on such as we,*
> *Baa! Yah! Bah!*[8]

This feeling of being "damned from here to Eternity," and consequently of being "lost souls," emerges from Kipling's own sense of alienation as an Anglo-Indian. This gave him a glimpse of the bleak abysmal recesses of their souls and the darkness of hell in which these gentlemen-rankers find themselves. It may not be quite valid to postulate any relationship between Kipling and existentialism, but one cannot escape the feeling that many of Kipling's poems, such as the one noted above, express a deep sense of existential suffering, the innermost pain of alienation and the slow movement toward death in an alien milieu. Kipling not only expressed, in this respect, the activistic ideals of British servicemen all over the world but also the tide of anguish which sweeps over them as a consequence of these ideals. Thus in Kipling's writings, activism as a normative value has inevitably a concomitant of anguish and suffering. But conversely, for Kipling action as a value is an antidote to the pain of isolation and alienation and thus becomes a sanctifying agency for a suffering soul.

In Kipling's creative cosmos activism operates as a dynamic source of inspiration. In *The Light that Failed* (1890), a moving novel of his early period, the frustrated hero, Dick Helder turns to war and a life of ceaseless activity as an escape from his gnawing sense of failure. His passion for Maisie becomes an instrument of destruction when he realizes that she is merely interested in her own career and not in sharing the joys and sorrows of his life. The light is failing as Dick is mysteriously becoming blind and he forces the doors of his isolated life open onto vast colonnades of heroic action. In a bid to make life meaningful, he proceeds to theaters of war, only to meet with death in Egypt. Dick knows that "one must do things and chart out life on a more purposive and activistist path," but the final solution eludes him as much as it eluded Kipling himself.

Similarly, Kipling's "The Galley-Slave" is a fine allegorical poem which could be described as a hymn of activism. The galley is described as "gallant" as those who man it. The galley-slaves are a "hard-bit gang," and though they are the servants of the sweep-head, yet they are the masters of the sea. The galley-slave, on the eve of his leaving the galley, exclaims:

> *God be thanked—whate'er comes after,*
> *I have lived and toiled with Men!* [9]

This is the accentuation of the feeling of action, devotion to duty and heroism of day-to-day, silent, glorious work. The galley-slaves also symbolically represent the privates, the government servants, civil and military, who sweat in the various offices of the government of India and who carry the burden of the responsibilities of administration. They jointly contribute to the action and work which are essential for the smooth functioning of the government bureaus.

Kipling's belief in the cardinal principle of activism sometimes finds expression in modes purely empirical. A life of action must necesarily pass through processes of trial and error. Kipling's emphasis on experience, and the empirical element involved in it, is therefore part of his credo. In actual life this doctrine of experience must be lived from day to day and, therefore, in Kipling's view the day's work assumes significance. The value of the day's work is thus in part activistic, and in part empirical, thereby forging an integrity of his vision of life.

The purposive application of energy to the enrichment of man's life and civilization is an essential element in Kipling's world view. The capacity for fruitful application of energy is a great quality of Western man and in Kipling's view the genius of the Anglo-Saxon race is expressed in it. Kipling therefore instinctively praises the work and qualities of persons who fill the ranks of the army and the civil service in India. Not that he is blind to their faults, but in a positive way he recognizes the contributions they make to the smooth operation of the governmental machine. Kipling uses the metaphor of the garden to pay tribute to England's men of action.

Our England is a garden, and such gardens are not made
By singing:—"Oh, how beautiful!" and sitting in the shade,
While better men than we go out and start their working
*   lives,*
At scrubbing weeds from granite paths with broken dinner-
*   knives.*
There's not a pair of legs as theirs, there's not a head so
*   thick,*
There's not a hand so weak and white, not yet a heart so sick,
But it can find some needful job that's crying to be done,
For the glory of the Garden glorifieth every one.[10]

The glory of the garden, that is England's green and pleasant land, arises out of the toil of its workingmen. Kipling exhorts his countrymen to "seek your job with thankfulness," and asks them to "work till further orders." This phrase, "work till further orders," smacks of officialese, and yet Kipling includes it in his poem because it glorifies his concept of the value of routine work.

Kipling, in endeavoring to give poetical expression to his activistic beliefs, forges a link between human work and divine blessings. In "My New-Cut Ashlar" he declares that all that is excellent in him is due to divine grace and that his failings are his own. Where he fails to meet God's thought, the blame is his. He then invokes God to bring "Eden to the craftsman's brain"

> The depth and dream of my desire,
> The bitter paths wherein I stray—
> Thou knowest Who hast made the Fire,
> Thou knowest Who hast made the Clay.
>
> Who, lest all thought of Eden fade,
> Bring'st Eden to the craftsman's brain—
> Godlike to muse o'er his own Trade
> And manlike stand with God again! [11]

In Kipling's view the concept of the craftsman's work thus assumes a god-like proportion because even the most commonplace work of man is inspired by the divine design. Kipling declared: "I saw nought common on Thy Earth." The earthy in Kipling's cosmos thus becomes heavenly, and the business of God's handiwork is projected upon the day's work of man on the earth.

Any assessment of Kipling's activism necessarily implies consideration of his imperialism which forms a significant facet of his doctrine. No student of Kipling's activism can afford to evade its implications or close his eyes ambivalently to this complex problem since it is central to Kipling's fictional world. But criticism of this aspect of his creative imagination ranges between extreme points of view, bordering on the barren land of clichés on the one hand and verging on the unexplored land of courageous defenses on the other.

For some critics, Kipling's imperialism is intolerably jingoistic, while for others it is a powerful myth with which he was
able to unify and imaginatively order his experience.

The tone and temper of Kipling's writings lend themselves
to diverse comments since whatever he wrote bears the stamp
not only of his felt experience but also of the wider intellectual issues of the day. The doctrine of imperialism as such
has become a useful critical tool in the hands of indiscrim-
inate critics with which to denounce Kipling. For instance,
an anonymous review in *Contemporary Review* is typical of
this type of mudslinging: "The exaltation to a position of
almost unexampled popularity of a writer who in his single
person adumbrates, I think, all that is most deplorable, all
that is most retrograde and savage in the restless and unin-
structed Hooliganism of the time . . . Mr. Rudyard Kipling." [12] Similarly, Wilhelm Dening felt that Kipling should
be regarded as a "wicked example of all that is negative in
England." [13] Generally critics thus tend to correlate all violence and savagery with Kipling's imperialistic doctrine. Hannah Arendt, for instance, considered Kipling to be "the author of the imperialist legend," [14] who created in the public
mind the image of the imperialist character. For H. E.
Bates all of Kipling's work is colored by imperialism and the
heroics of his era.[15] Nelson Bushnell went a step further and
declared with enviable nonchalance that Kipling helped build
the creed of imperialism based on the blind assumption of
superiority to "the basic lack of understanding of what are
called 'the lesser breeds' and their point of view." [16]

Against this critical debunking we have spririted defenses.
Charles Carrintgon defends Kipling against all attacks of
"imperialistic trends" and suggests that the main theme of
Kipling's fiction is "seldom caste, class or imperialism seen
from a single prejudice, but moral issues." [17] Similarly, Bonamy Dobrée suggests that Kipling's imperialism is not
chauvinistic and that it symbolizes compassion, not hate.[18]
Kipling's concern is with the "healing of horror" rather than
with horror itself, in its unmitigated callousness.

One may thus list scores of critical comments expressing
an adverse judgment on Kipling's imperialistic attitude and

juxtapose them wth spirited defenses against this massive critical assault. But mere mapping out of adverse or favorable attitudes will not resolve the issue, for the subject of dispute is far more complex than is readily apparent. Kipling's mind was molded by the extant intellectual and political doctrines and therefore one of the ways to disentangle this problem is to place it in its historical context.

Kipling's imperialist attitude sprang from diverse beliefs which were in part racial and political and in part moral and religious. The early Kipling's outlook was molded by many contemporary notions regarding the "superiority" of the Anglo-Saxon race. It is rather ironic that the publication of Charles Darwin's *The Origin of Species* (1859), regarded as a pioneering work in biology and a decisive landmark in the development of science, reinforced the attitude of racial superiority of the whites against the blacks or of the Europeans against the Asians and Africans. The racialist approach to history received, it was felt, scientific authenticity from the Darwinian concept of the survival of the fittest in the growth and evolution of races. It is also curious that Darwin's great work was published only two years after the Great Uprising of 1857 in India,[19] which is described by British historians as the Great Mutiny and by recent Indian historians as the first Great War of Independence. Whatever may be the mode of describing the event, the fact remains that the Indian rebels were defeated by the superior force of British arms in India. This military defeat of the Indians was construed as another important piece of evidence in support of the racial and political preeminence of the British. This argument, however, is manifestly naïve since it overlooks the fact that a majority of those who fought for the East India Company and secured the victory of the British power over Indian rebels were themselves Indians. In any case, there can be little doubt that contemporary political events in India strengthened the British imperialistic attitude. Although it was conceded that the British Empire in India was one of the accidents of history, acquired almost in a "fit of absent-mindedness," as the Empire grew in stature, it became a focal point for the assumption of racial and intellectual superiority. As Donald C. Gordon has pointed out:

Perhaps the explanation for British power that was most likely to justify a permanent British *Raj* in India was the notion "that British power in India was based on some special characteristics of the British people," or in the more popular language of the day, on the unique qualities of the Anglo-Saxon race.[20]

This sense of supremacy was the source of the imperialistic stance of nineteenth-century England. It is mirrored in, for example, Joseph Chamberlain's belief that "the British race is the greatest of governing races that the world has ever seen." Cecil Rhodes, a friend of Kipling, believed that the British were "the best people in the world," with their steadfast devotion to democracy and justice. Similarly, Lord Grover thought that the British in extending their dominion on the face of the earth, were fulfilling the mission of a truly Christian civilization.

Kipling's attitude to the British Empire is an extraordinary combination of myth and reality. For him, the Empire was a legend and a part of this strange mythos. In a lecture to the officers of an East Coast Patrol in 1918 Kipling spoke about the foundation legend of the British Isles [21] and the expanding Empire. According to him, the British Isles are surrounded by the sea on all sides and crave the help of the three elements of Water, Air, and Sun for survival. The achievement of the British is symbolized by their skill in shipbuilding, and the ship becomes the symbol of their expanding power over the oceans and lands of the earth. England is a ship of state steered by her many wise and valiant captains through long ages of her journey. The ship was also the primary means of England's conquest of India and other territories in the world.

The enterprising and ambitious Englishmen moved to different parts of the world in a tremendous bid for the expansion of their Empire. They felt that their task was not mere conquest, but the gradual realization of the progress of backward peoples and inferior races. This is the essence of the "white man's burden" that Kipling eulogized in a specific context. Their mission was neither purely military, nor was it purely political. It was essentially moral. Therefore, in Kipling's imagination, the British empire-builder was only a modern and real version of the mystical dragon-slayer of Greek legends. In this way the political, the religious, and the moral approaches are strangely mixed in Kipling's formulation of the concept of the Empire.

The concepts of the dragon-slayer and the reformer of backward peoples are vividly expressed in an absorbing story, "The Tomb of His Ancestors" in *The Day's Work* (1898). It describes the career of John Chinn, who goes to India to join his father's regiment. His grandfather, too, had served in India and worked among the tribe known as *Bhils*. These Bhils and Bukta, a native officer, believed that John Chinn was a reincarnation of his grandfather since his birthmark, manner of speech, and physical endurance were similar to those of his deceased grandfather. When a project to vaccinate the Bhils was launched, there was opposition to it and the rumor spread that the dead grandfather was riding in the hills on a clouded tiger. The colonel of the regiment asked John Chinn how he could control the Bhils' unrest and persuade them to accept vaccination, and John says:

> I've got a sort of hereditary influence over 'em. . . . It's rather rummy. It seems, from what I can make out that I'm my own grandfather reincarnated, and I've been disturbing the peace of the country by riding a pad-tiger of nights.[22]

John Chinn and Bukta spent the night near the ancestral tomb and, like a modern dragon's slayer, John shot the tiger-horse as evidence of his good faith. As a man devoted to progress, he also persuaded the Bhils to be vaccinated. In this way, the story of John Chinn and the "Tomb of His Ancestors" dramatizes the myth and reality of the Empire. The story, the language, the development of the narrative have a sweeping movement, which is also the way the British Empire spread over the globe in the eighteenth and nineteenth centuries.

Similarly, in "The Song of the Dead," Kipling is eulogizing the sacrifices of the English in the cause of the expansion of the Empire:

We have fed our sea for a thousand years
  And she calls us, still unfed,
Though there's never a wave or all her waves
  But marks our English dead:
We have strawed our best to the weed's unrest,
  To the shark and the sheering gull
If blood be the price of admiralty,
  Lord God, we ha' paid in full!

There's never a flood goes shoreward now
  But lifts a keel we manned;
There's never an ebb goes seaward now
  But drops our dead on the sand—
But slinks our dead on the sands forlore,
  From the Ducies to the Swin.
If blood be the price of admiralty,
If blood be the price of admiralty,
  Lord God, we ha' paid it in! [23]

Kipling believes that the English must continue to feed the sea with their bodies and souls for "that is our doom and pride." He invokes the memory of Drake to pay glowing tribute to those pioneers and adventurers on the high seas who become the empire builders of Britannia. The empire builders in tropical countries and on the frontier are confronted with a new arithmetic of life. They learn that even very expensive and exclusive education is no proof against an ordinary rifle.

No proposition Euclid wrote
  No formulae the text-books know
Will turn the bullet from your coat. [24]

Kipling is quite conscious of the fluid arithmetic of life which an empire builder must learn and live with, however, great and fearful the dangers to which he is exposed. Kipling attempts to weave the psychology of sacrifice into the fabric of the daily lives of soldiers and servicemen who staff the outposts of the empire. In "The Story of Uriah" he presents a modern version of the killing of Uriah in the battle at the behest of David, who had fallen in love with Uriah's wife, Bathsheba. Thus Jack Barrett, who was posted to Quetta, died at that outpost of Britain's Indian Empire and he never understood the reasons for his transfer. He had left his wife at Simla and she mourned for him "five lively months at most." This offers a parallelism to Bathsheba's mourning for Uriah Hittite: "And when the wife of Uriah heard that Uriah her husband was dead, she mourned for her husband." But soon David fetched Bathsheba who became his wife. Kipling does not make the irony of Jack Barrett's life explicit, but the biblical parallel sets the tone of this simple poem. It also suggests that Kipling, however proud he may be of the positive achievements of the empire builders, is not really blind to their weak spots and moral degeneration. In fact, "Arithmetic on the Frontier" is a bitter criticism of the stupidity and vileness of the administrators of the British *Raj* in India, not only in terms of posting Jack Barrett at Quetta, but also of wasting men and material in defending a border which is so uncertain and unstable. Kipling is, indirectly, calling into question the whole imperialistic strategy of defending the indefensible.

Therefore, if on the one hand Kipling projects his romantic concept of the Empire, it must be said that he is also very critical of negative empire builders on the other. His romantic image of the Empire is ruined by many harsh and cruel realities, and what needs to be especially stressed is that Kipling is not blind to these actualities. In "Gentlemen-Rankers" Kipling exposes the dreadful story of the gentlemen who "dance with blowzy housemaids at the regimental hops" and thrash a cad "who says you waltz too well." He is consciously exposing the horror of their fall. In "Private Ortheris's Song," in *Life's Handicap*, the soldier confesses that he "went on the drunk" and then he "went to the bad." Kipling makes the private look into himself: "My very worst friend from beginning to end. By the blood of a mouse was myself!" The later phase of Kipling's career was increasingly marked by a sense of disillusionment with the way his concept of the Empire was being devalued and degenerated by men and events, especially after the Boer War.

In the earlier phase Kipling evolved his concept of the "white man's burden," which became a moral and cultural concomitant of the political value of the Empire. However, it is neither desirable nor is it valid to artificially impose any sense of uniformity on Kipling's varied and fluid approaches to imperialism. He almost creates a mystique of the Empire and in this mythical world high moral ideals are mixed up with objectives of material progress. The concept of the white man's burden is part of this mythos. The Hymn, the "White Man's Burden," was addressed to the United States on the eve of its control over the Philippines in 1899, and its tone is set by the inspiring exhortation offered by an Anglo-Saxon bard to the new English-speaking nation across the Atlantic. Kipling earnestly believed in the mission of the white races in civilizing backward peoples of the world because he believed that educationally, scientifically, and technologically they were well equipped to carry out this mission. This great hymn had a negative as well as a positive response and became a bone of contention between Tories and Liberals. Kipling urged Americans to understand their destiny and act on their ideals. Theodore Roosevelt, who sent a copy of the poem to Henry Cabot Lodge in 1899, said that it was "rather poor poetry" but "good sense" [25] from the practical, political point of view.

Although Kipling had declared that the "White Man's Burden" was no "tawdry rule of Kings" and that ironically the white man might "reap his old reward," that is, the hate and the blame of those "ye guard," yet even the positive elements in Kipling's concept came under a fiery attack. As Bonamy Dobrée has pointed out, the phrase "White Man's Burden" itself, in liberal circles, "gave scope for glowing self-righteousness and the laughter of contempt." [26] The Liberals were outraged by the pomposity and pride of Kipling's attitude, and even though the facts he stated were not altogether wrong, the perspectives and approaches emanating from them were positively painful.

The concept of the white man's burden is, indeed, part of Kipling's philosophy of life. His attitude is one of acceptance of responsibility, of the call of stern duty in the face of the dangers of anarchy and misrule. However, he seems to reject limpid altruism as the idle dream of misguided idealists. He appears equally opposed to the "sentimental" notions of equality and fraternity loudly proclaimed by Rousseau and the ideas of radicalism or internationalism which came in the wake of the French Revolution. Kipling's philosophy of life is nourished by his strong British Methodist background which inspired him to formulate firm moral attitudes. This lends strength and toughness to his philosophy.

Kipling's notion of the white man's burden was also religious and moral. It was essentially a call to moral duty, the stern daughter of God. The British Whigs, like Chamberlain and Hobson, agreed that the only justification for Britain's Empire was its contribution to the civilization of the world. Lord Curzon stated that he found, in the Empire not merely the key to glory and wealth, but also "the call to duty, and 'the means of service' to mankind." [27]

This concept of duty and steadfast devotion to the cause was central to British imperialism in India and it passed from one generation to the other. It is interesting to observe the reactions of Jawaharlal Nehru, an inveterate enemy of British imperialism, to this aspect of its growth. He said that the British approach to Indian problems "fascinated while it irritated" and that their calm assurance in face of the greatest provocation aroused mixed reactions. His comment that "there was something of the religious temper about this attitude" [28] is particularly meaningful since it is only the other side of what Kipling was trying to present. The adverse critics of the concept of imperialism accused its advocates of clever "phrase-mongering" and using "masked words." "The White Man's Burden" is, in their view, an example of this credulous phrase-mongering.

Kipling's concept of the white man's burden can, therefore, be interpreted very differently from what his most adverse critics have done. In fact, it could be considered, according to Richard Cook, as one of Kipling's saving graces, and it is important to realize how deep Kipling's belief was in this moral-religious-reformist concept. Kipling genuinely believed that the primary aim of the Empire was the spread and enrichment of civilization. Any balanced history of the British Empire in the nineteenth century will indicate, *inter alia*, its many benevolent as well as its destructive aspects. Kipling's empire builders are marked by a deep moral consciousness, which is almost totally absent in modern twentieth-century empire builders of totalitarian regimes. His attitude to the colored peoples was certainly one of superiority, but it was not without the emotion of love. He regards them with love and parental solicitude, though he is conscious of their inferiority and imperviousness to the law. In "Recessional," for instance, Kipling's tone is one of strong rebuke of the British because they are swerving from their righteous path. Then again, the law is not a close preserve or the sole monopoly of the British alone. It is purely a moral concept which even the non-British people may imbibe and thereby give a better account of themselves than what the British have done. The British happen to embody the law in the nineteenth century but, in Kipling's vision, the future is very much open.

Thus Kipling's view of the Empire is romantic, sentimental and idealistic. The Kiplingesque variety of imperialism is far more preferable than the aggressive imperialism of some of the Socialist or Communist or totalitarian countries today. In any event, the nineteenth-century British imperialism was far less oppressive than the imperialism of other European powers in African and Asian countries. Kipling's Empire is not really dark and dismal. But he projected with firm moral determination his own idealistic and moral concepts on what the British Empire in the nineteenth century really was.

Imperialism kindled only one side of Kipling's primary and pervasive imagination and the other side explored his thirst for the primitive and the primordial in man. This twofold process of the operation of his imagination is exemplified in his well-known polo story, "The Maltese Cat." [29] The cat is the principal pony in the Skidars' team engaged in a match against the Archangels. Lutyens, the owner, trusted the Maltese cat to win the match and the Cup, which it did. The Maltese cat later joined the victory celebrations where **it** "was petted all round the table" [30] and the people drank its health since it had done more than any man or horse to win the Cup. In this lovely tale of the Maltese cat the two elements in Kipling's imagination are operative. His two souls are reflected in the delicate prismatic story. He is an imperialistic Anglo-Saxon settled in India and the setting of the club substantiates this element. His imagination is kindled by the beauty and charm of India, and his love for the primitive and the mysterious finds full expression in the delicate and sensitive treatment of the pony and the game and the relationship between Lutyen and the Maltese cat. Thus, imperialism is no longer a dry and hybrid doctrine and when it serves as a source of Kipling's imagination, it is suffused with his love for the primordial in man.

Kipling's concept of the Empire is part of his belief in activism as a philosophy of life. Kipling visualized, under the impact of Spinoza, a theory of life in which the doctrine of experience and the doctrine of action both play a vital part. He delighted in the *doing* of things and one must concede that his empire builders were primarily men of action whose lives were enriched by varied experience of the wide world which they traversed. But the activist in Kipling is transformed into an artist and his activistic concept of the Empire is transformed into a mystique. This mystique of the Empire becomes as large as life itself and equally baffling and inexplicable. Kipling's philosophy of life thus finds expression in his activism and imperialism. But he is also obsessed by the darkness within, the darkness of hell which alienates him from the main path of his credo. Therefore, the vision of Kipling the artist is expressed through his alienated activism and imperialism.

3

Kim

Kim is the profoundest expression of Kipling's creative talent. It is not only the climax of his artistic development, but also a culmination of the process of Becoming which is woven into the texture of his work. Kipling seems to be preoccupied all along with an attempt to achieve a poise—an equilibrium —between the two divergent phenomena of Being and Becoming. From this perspective, *Kim* represents Kipling's innate quest for selfhood. It is true that the activist in Kipling seems always to be in conflict with the quietist and he seems to be engaged in the dual processes of Being and Becoming almost simultaneously. But in *Kim* the accent is on the transition from Being to Becoming. Kim makes an intense effort, at least in one direction, to change his identity, his modes of behavior, in pursuance of his obsession with "the other self." *Kim*, as Mark Kinkead-Weekes has pointed out, "is an expression of what Keats called 'negative capability.'"[1] This is true since *Kim* represents Kipling's attempt to transcend the boundaries of his self in quest of a new identity. He wished to become, as it were, what he was not himself, thereby experiencing and expressing a process of Becoming.

This process of Becoming, as expressed in *Kim*, demonstrates the all-inclusive and composite nature of Kipling's artistic vision. But this centrality of vision which is at the heart of Kipling's art is generally ignored since *Kim* is structurally episodic in character. Moreover, the "spy" element of the story has misled many critics to regard the novel as merely an absorbing sequence of thrilling incidents evoking

a strange but real world. This resulted, by and large, in dis-
regarding the complicated pattern of experience woven round
the basic mode of Becoming. If this core of Kipling's vision
as embodied in *Kim* is not properly perceived, the real significance of the novel may elude the reader. Writing on the
critical neglect in this regard, Nirad C. Chaudhuri has
pointed out:

> I wonder if, in spite of their great love for it, Englishmen
> have quite understood what *Kim* is about. It has often
> been read piecemeal, as every great story can be, for its
> details evocative either of the Himalayas or of the Indo-
> Gangetic plain. These are so interesting and gripping that
> the reader hardly feels the need for a larger unifying
> theme, and does not take the trouble to look for it.[2]

Kipling's art in *Kim* is thus deceptively episodic and almost
kaleidoscopic. Kim's sojourn on the Grand Trunk Road,
depicting the ever fluctuating pattern of his experience, is
adduced, though wrongly, as evidence of the lack of unifying
theme. This only shows the failure to realize the central unity
of the novel stemming from the hero's sense of Becoming.
The kaleidoscopic variety of scene and action not only represents the "process" of Kim's evolution into selfhood, but also
underscores the basic unity which gives a sense of together-
ness to the various components of the novel. *Kim* is, thus, an
organic whole of many parts with a unifying theme emerging
from the process of the protagonist's Becoming.

It is interesting to observe how *Kim* has been misunder-
stood by critics at the turn of the century. *Kim* abounded,
one reviewer declared, "in the rather brutal energy some of
Mr. Kipling's admirers love."[3] Another reviewer said, "We
would have admired Kim's good qualities if he were a
cleaner hero."[4] A third commentator thought it was a kind
of primer of patriotism and taught "the notion that physical
strength and the love of domination constitute heroism."[5]
Another reviewer wrote that the novel "is less a connected
whole than a string of incidents."[6] J. H. Miller reviewing
Kim emphasized the kaleidoscopic quality of Kipling's art.
The character of Kim, he said, was a "masterly conception."[7]

but it is neither in the fable (exciting and ingenious though it may be) nor in the portrayal of character (however skillful and convincing) that the charm of *Kim* rests. Its secret lies in the wonderful "panorama it unrolls before us of the life of the great Peninsula over whose government England has now presided for more than a century." It is in this context, but in a different perspective, that Edmund Wilson has criticized the "imperialistic strain" in *Kim*.

> Now what the reader tends to expect is that Kim will come eventually to realise that he is delivering into bondage to the British invaders those whom he has always considered his own people, and that a struggle between allegiances will result.[8]

Kim, says Edmund Wilson, engages in activities which constitute a betrayal of the cause of the lama. A. B. Maurice attacked *Kim* as "cold, dead, and lifeless," [9] whereas T. S. Eliot thought it was "Kipling's greatest book." [10] In Boris Ford's view, *Kim* is a mere boy's tale of adventure.

> This novel is so disarmingly superficial that even its less pleasant elements, those relating to the colour conflict, fail to give any sharp offence.[11]

These conflicting views and judgments only highlight the truth that *Kim* is not a simple novel. It is not just a "Secret Service" romance or a mere "spy drama," but quite a complex work of art. Its apparent simplicity of narration and description has presumably deceived many critics into formulating and expressing oversimplified, one-sided judgments.

All the component elements of *Kim*—the story and the plot, the texture and the structure, the theme and the symbol—contribute to its rich complexity. There is a perfect fusion of theme and structure. But central to the overall design of the novel is Kim's search for selfhood and the resultant process of Becoming. Kim himself articulates this unmistakably: "'I am Kim. I am Kim; and what is Kim?' His soul repeated it again and again." [12] This quest for the real self, this obsession to know oneself, is the key to the structural and thematic significance of *Kim* as a novel. The paradoxical nature of Kim's quest—poised between the assertion of identity and the questioning of that identity—gives the novel an element of ambiguity which is in tune with the fluctuating nature of Kim's self-awareness. He asserts that he is Kim and yet questions "what is Kim?" (The choice of the pronoun "what" instead of "who" suggests this ambiguity.) This loss of identity is suggested by Kipling in another context through the image of the cogwheel. Describing Kim's sense of the loss of a meaningful milieu Kipling says that he is "a cog-wheel unconnected with any machinery, just like idle cog-wheel of a cheap Beheea sugar-crusher." This picture of the mechanical cogwheel that is Kim's self is paralleled by the concept of the Wheel of Life of the lama.

Kim revolves around this basic process of Becoming, of Kim's search for identity. It is not easy, therefore, to do justice to this theme by a mere summary of the story, since the novel has a complicated pattern indicative of the multiple levels of reality in which it operates. Yet an analysis of the main events is an indispensable preliminary for its interpretation. The story of *Kim* seems curiously simple and vital. Kim, the hero, is an orphan child. His father, an Irish soldier, and his mother, an Irish nurse, are dead. Kim grows up among Indian children, Hindu and Muslim boys, in Lahore and is well conversant with the language and modes of behavior of Indians.

In chapter 1 Kim is introduced as sitting across the famous old gun Zam-Zammah, the "fire-breathing dragon" on a brick platform opposite the Lahore Museum in that picturesque city of the Punjab. Kim's mother was a nursemaid in a colonel's family. She had married Kimball O'Hara, a young sergeant of the Mavericks, an Irish regiment. The mother died of cholera in Ferozepore and Kimball became an alcoholic. He, at the head of a grand Irish regiment with "nine hundred first-class devils" would attend on Kim. It was foretold by his father that Kim would cross the way of the Irish regiment, the crest of which was "a Red Bull on a green field." Kim readily believed in this prophecy and so did the woman who reared him.

As Kim played with his friend, Abdullah, he spotted a

Tibetan lama "nearly six feet high, dressed in fold upon fold of dingy stuff." The lama told Kim that he "came by Kulu— from beyond the Kailas—" and that he was a "follower of the Middle Way," living in the quiet atmosphere of his lamasery and wished to see the "Four Holy Places" before his death. Kim offered to show the lama the Lahore Museum, the Wonder House or the "Ajaib-Gher." The lama was greatly impressed with the Greco-Buddhist sculptures in the museum. He half sobbed at the sight of the great Buddha: "The Lord! The Lord! It is Sakya Muni himself." In the museum the lama met the curator, an Englishman of wide learning in archaeology and the arts, and had a curious conversation about Lord Buddha and breaking of the Bow. The Lord, the lama said, shot an arrow, and it fell on a spot where a river began to flow. It was the lama's life mission to discover this "River of the Arrow," as it was sacred to Buddhism. The curator knew Buddhist religion and history, but wouldn't precisely answer the lama's key question: "Where is that river, Fountain of Wisdom, where fell the arrow?" "Alas, my brother, I do not know," said the curator. The lama, then, outlined the intended course to seek the Divine Law and declared that he would first visit the temple of the Tirthankers in Benares, then Buddha Gaya, Kapilavastu, and, finally, the great River of the Arrow. The curator presented to the lama a pair of crystal spectacles and the lama in return gave the curator an antique iron pencase.

Kim was greatly excited by this extraordinary encounter between the lama and the curator and the possibilities of his accompanying the lama on the journey. The lama's *chela,* or disciple, had died and he was looking for another *chela.* Kim then accompanied the lama, accepting "this new God [Buddhist] without emotion." The lama told Kim that he begged for his food and the new *chela* offered to beg for him loudly and knowingly: "Those who beg in silence starve in silence." Kim trotted off to a vegetable-seller and by catching "on his moist blue nose" the Brahminee bull that was about to wreck the shop, procured hot, steaming rice and curry from the shopkeeper for the lama. Kim was amazed when the lama told him that a boy had come to him at the Wonder House, "in place of him who died," to show him a road which he had lost. Then Kim offered to help the lama in his search for the River of the Arrow. The lama asked animatedly: "Who art thou?" " 'Thy *chela*,' said Kim simply, sitting on his heels." Then Kim told him of his own search for a "Red Bull on a green field." The lama and Kim both moved on to Kashmir Serai where they met Mahbub Ali, who was a horse-dealer, a "big burly Afghan," hailing from the "mysterious land beyond the Passes of the North." Kim told Mahbub that he would go with the lama to Benares and Mahbub asked him to carry a message to the British officer at Umballa: "The pedigree of the white stallion is fully established." Mahbub's name was registered as a spy in the locked books of the Indian Survey Department as C.25.IB, and he was also carrying information from another spy, R.17, from beyond the Dora Pass. Mahbub asked Kim to deliver the message because he "was the one soul in the world who had never told him a lie." Mahbub then visited a dancing girl and drank a great deal. Meanwhile his quarters were searched by persons who suspected him of transmitting secret messages. Kim silently observed the turbaned Delhi man searching even the soles of Mahbub's slippers but to no avail. Kim and the lama left the Serai for Benares.

In chapter 2 Kim and the lama board the 3:25 A.M. south-bound *te-rain* for Amritzar and Umballa. Kim's encounter with the "booking devil" when getting his ticket showed his practical sense and awareness of the corrupt practices in Asia. Kim and the lama met interesting people on the *te-rain*, the Hindu Jat, his wife, and the Amritzar courtesan, who was generous enough to buy tickets and food for Kim. While the lama talked of the River of the Arrow, Kim spoke of the Red Bull on a green field, as their main objectives. At Umballa the cultivator's wife offered lodgings to the lama and Kim. Kim stole out alone and visited Colonel Creighton's bunga-low in accordance with the directions given by Mahbub Ali. He slipped through the garden hedge and hid himself in shrubs and as soon as an Englishman appeared he passed on Mahbub's cryptic message: "The pedigree of the white stallion is fully established." Creighton asked for the proof and Kim flipped the wad of folded paper into the air. Creighton picked it up and dropped a rupee for Kim. Kim stayed and watched the house and heard of military preparations involving eight thousand men. He also learnt that the commander in chief was on a visit to Creighton's and that telegrams would be sent soon ordering the troops to march. Kim returned to the cultivator's home and found the lama and the local priest talking about horoscopes. The priest declared that Kim's prophecy would be fulfilled in the next three days. The lama and Kim left Umballa. Their hosts gave Kim a large "bundle of good food" and watched him and the lama go southward in the dawn.

In chapter 3 the lama and Kim had a brief encounter with a gardener who considered them unwelcome beggars but later discovered that the tall priest was only searching for a river. Kim spotted a big snake, a cobra with "fixed, lidless eyes" and wished to break its back with a stick. The lama commented that the cobra too "is upon the Wheel as we are — a life ascending or descending — very far from deliverance." The lama asked the cobra whether it knew of the river, a scene which completely baffled Kim since he shared the Englishman's abomination for the snake. They stayed with a soldier who had fought in the Mutiny of 1857, and they discussed the prospects of finding the river of healing. Kim prophesied the war, while the old soldier directed them to the Grand Trunk Road: "And truly the Grand Trunk Road is a wonderful spectacle. It runs straight, bearing without crowding India's traffc for fifteen hundred miles — such a river of life as exists nowhere else in the world."

In chapter 4 the lama and Kim continued their journey. They met the son of an old soldier who told them that his regiment was under orders for a probable war. The father said, "Ho! Friend of all the World, a war is toward as thou hast said!" Kipling gives a magnificent account of the activities on the Grank Trunk Road bustling with life, energy, and vitality. The variegated life and lovely scenes on the Road are vividly portrayed. Kim and the lama come across an old lady of Kulu, hailed as the "Great Queen," and her impressive retinue, comprising "thin-legged, gray-bearded

Ooryas from down country" and "duffle-clad . . . hillmen of the North." She talked to Kim and desired a meeting with the holy lama. The lama met her and found her a virtuous and wise woman. She invited them to join her men on the journey to Buddh-Gaya but she had not heard the great truths of the river nor did she know the story of the arrow. The great woman of Kulu, who is the embodiment of benevolence and charity, narrated them tales of local gods.

In chapter 5 the procession got under way and came to a halting stage. The lama thought that the lady from Kulu was a wise and discerning woman but that it was hard to meditate in her proximity. The lama and Kim walked away from the procession and saw white soldiers preparing a camp with flags—the Red Bull on the green field. As Kim saw the soldiers, he gasped, "O Holy One! My horoscope!" He recalled the prophecy of the priest that two messengers would appear in a dark place. The white soldiers belonged to the Irish regiment of Kim's father, the Mavericks, whose crest was the great Red Bull on a background of Irish green. The Mavericks had their Church of England chaplain, Bennett, who on seeing Kim presumed that he was stealing. But the boy spoke English, and Bennett got hold of the charm that hung around Kim's neck and called Father Victor, the Roman Catholic chaplain, for advice. They found the clue in Kim's baptismal certificate and knew that he was the son of Kimball O'Hara, formerly of the Mavericks. Kimball had scribbled: "Look after the boy. Please look after the boy." Father Victor concluded that O'Hara's boy was in league with all the powers of Darkness, whereas Kim declared that his search for the Red Bull on the green field was now over. Bennett and Victor discussed Kim's future and told the lama that the regiment would take care of the boy. The lama was genuinely distressed at the inevitable parting of ways between him and Kim, though the boy assured him he would help the holy man in his search for the River. The lama said that those who "follow the Way" must not surrender to the fire of any desire or attachment because it is all illusion. He approved the idea of sending Kim to a good school, and inquired about the cost of education. He was told that St.

Xavier's at Lucknow was an excellent school and the cost might be between two to three hundred rupees a year. The lama took down Father Victor's address and resumed his journey. Kim then told Bennett of the threat of the impending war and the "little imp" was handed over to a sergeant, who would look after him. Kim told the sergeant: "Eight thousand men, besides guns. . . . Very soon you will see."

In chapter 6 the Mavericks, after dismantling their tents, moved on to Umballa. Kim discovered that he was being closely watched by Father Victor and Mr. Bennett. The colonel received orders for marching to the front and was taken aback by Kim's prophecy coming true. Kim was praised for his prophecy and became "an object of distinguished consideration." The regiment left Umballa and Kim was left behind in empty barracks in charge of a drummer-boy. In the barracks an angry schoolmaster tried to stuff Kim's head with the alphabet and figures. Kim resisted all formal schooling and considered poisoning the schoolmaster. He loathed the drummer-boy and managed to send for a professional letter-writer and dispatch a letter to Mahbub Ali, the horse-dealer. A minor encounter between the drummer-boy and Kim showed that he was thoroughly unaware of life in England and disliked the coldness and indifference of the life of the whites.

Father Victor sent for Kim and read to him the letter received from the lama, stating that "Education is greatest blessing" and that Kim was the "apple" of his eye and that "rupees shall be sent per hoondi three hundred per annum." While Father Victor was worried over the prospects of Kim being brought up in accordance with the tenets of the Church of England or being sent to St. Xavier's for a better education, Kim saw nothing of this dilemma but only the vision of the lama traveling south in a train. Father Victor was baffled by Kim's beguiling nature and strange ways of thinking and acting. The priest's discomfiture was accentuated by the drummer-boy's account of Kim suddenly disappearing with a "nigger on horseback." Kim was taken to the racecourse by Mahbub Ali, where he met Colonel Creighton. The conversation between Kim and Mahbub Ali revealed how deeply the Afghan horse-dealer was attached to the boy whom he and the lama called "the Friend of all the World." Both Mahbub Ali and Creighton thought that Kim, with his excellent grasp of native modes and knowledge of Hindustani, could be an excellent recruit to the British Secret Service in India—known as the "Game." Father Victor and Creighton met and discussed Kim's prospects. It was decided that he should go to Lucknow to St. Xavier's, and Mahbub Ali assured Kim that "thy fortune is made."

In chapter 7 Kim is shown dictating a letter to the lama saying that he would be going to school at "Nucklao." He met Creighton again and then traveled to Lucknow to enter the school. The colonel had a long talk with Kim in fluent and picturesque Urdu suggesting that he was to "enter the Survey of India as a chainman." Kim knew quite well that this promised job of thirty rupees a month was really connected with the British Secret Service. Kim realized that when he would become a chainman he would be employed by the colonel in the same way in which he was used by Mahbub Ali. The city of Lucknow held great charm for Kim—a fair city, a beautiful city, a rich city. As Kim was being taken in a coach to the school, his eye caught a figure near the wall. It was the lama who had arrived from Benares to meet him. Kim asked the lama why he did not stay with the Kulu woman and the holy man replied that his main purpose was the search for the River of the Arrow. The meeting between the lama and Kim reveals their deep involvement in each other, although the holy man disclaimed having been "misguided by the red mist of affection." Kim told him that his heart was in the letter he wrote to the lama and that, save Mahbub Ali and the lama, he had no friends in this world. The lama wiped his tears and expressed the hope that Kim would turn out to be as great a "Fountain of Wisdom" as the curator. Kim began to weep as the lama departed for the Temple of the Tirthankers at Benares. The lama asked Kim not to shed tears at their separation because all "desire is illusion and a new binding upon the Wheel."

Kim entered the school and made reasonably good progress

in education, though he was teased by his schoolmates. During the holidays he decided to take to the road again, instead of going to a barrack school. With the help of a *naikan*, a woman of easy virtue, he disguised himself as a "nigger." Creighton, who was at Simla, was told that young Kim had disappeared from Lucknow. But Mahbub Ali was in town and he met Creighton and the colonel heard the story of the raid on Kashmir Serai and Kim's role in it. Mahbub's view of Kim's adventure was that "the pony learns the game" and that "the great game" must be played by Kim alone. Kim decided to go with Mahbub Ali to Umballa.

In chapter 8 the close relationship between Mahbub Ali and Kim is revealed. Kim changed his dress and looked "externally at least, a Mohammedan." Kim explained to Mahbub Ali why he ran away from school. "Why should I not run away when the school was shut?" Kim then told Mahbub how he saw the commander in chief coming to dinner at Creighton's and how he got the news. He promised Mahbub that he would attend the school, but that during holidays he must be free to "go among my people." "And who are thy people, O Friend of all the World?" "This great and beautiful land," said Kim. This is a meaningful statement. While talking to Mahbub Ali about the customs of Sahibs and the folks of Hind, Kim paused and reflected. "What am I? Mussalman, Hindu, Jain, or Buddhist? That is a hard knot." Kim found the two men who wanted to attack Mahbub Ali and the police arrested them.

In chapter 9 Kim was on his way, "upon the next turn of the wheel," to the house of Lurgan Sahib, an English shopkeeper, with whom he would be lodged until his return to school. He met a Hindu boy on the street who guided him to Lurgan's house, which was full of Tibetan devil-dance masks of awful terror. Lurgan asked Kim to sleep in the room crowded with masks. Kim guessed that his nerves were being tested but he was more afraid of the soft-eyed Hindu child than the ghastly and awful masks. The Hindu boy became jealous of Kim, tried to kill him and poison Lurgan. "A genuine imported Sahib from England would have made a great to do over this tale," but Lurgan responded to it in a carefree, native manner. Kim was hypnotized and under that spell played the "jewel game"—sometimes with stones, sometimes with swords and daggers, sometimes with photographs. Lurgan was interested in religion and discussed metaphysics with Bengali Babus. He had great expertise in makeup, and Kim was dressed up by Lurgan in various costumes.

Kim met Hurree Chunder Mookerjee, who was working for the Secret Service and was categorized under Ethnological Survey as R. 17. The Bengali Babu talked uninterruptedly on the advantages of education, learning Latin, Shakespeare and Wordsworth, Burke and Hare, and the art and science of mensuration. At the end of this long talk, he expressed his hope "to enjoy your [Kim's] offeecial acquaintance." *Ad interim*, he gave Kim a betel-box containing drugs. Hurree Chunder Mookerjee also escorted Kim to St. Xavier's. Kim registered steady progress at the school, for three years winning prizes in map making. The school records showed that Kim passed the examination in elementary surveying "with great credit." During the three years, the lama traveled widely in Southern India and also paid several visits to Lucknow to meet Kim. During the visits the lama ceased for a time mourning the loss of the River and talked of the beauty and wisdom of his *chela*.

Chapter 10 tells of Kim spending his holidays in "native garb" in Mahbub's company at Bombay. They returned by sea, visiting Karachi where Kim was invited to a Haj dinner. Kim experienced seasickness and pretended that he was poisoned. Lurgan taught Kim the Koran. On a visit to the "mysterious city of Bikaneer" Kim was presented with garments of great splendor and a .450 revolver by Mahbub Ali, who said, "Were I the Amir of Afghanistan . . . I would fill my mouth with gold." Creighton and Mahbub decided to allow Kim to go out with his red lama. Mahbub spoke of Hurree Babu's meetings with the lama, and Lurgan revealed the Babu's desire to be made a member of the Royal Society on the basis of ethnological notes. Creighton found a place for Kim as "an assistant chainman" in the

Canal Department for twenty rupees a month. Mahbub
took Kim to Huneefa, a blind woman, who applied dyestuff
to his skin as a protection on the road. Hurree Babu took
notes and talked of Spencer as Huneefa cast a spell, calling
upon devil after devil to keep away from dear Kim. Kim
received from her a secret amulet and passwords. Hurree
Babu accompanied Kim to the Lucknow railroad station
". . . and was gone." Kim found himself thoroughly
equipped for his journey on the road.

In Chapter 11 Kim came across a long-haired Hindu holy
man and talked to him about the road to Enlightenment,
thereby dispelling his over-powering sense of loneliness. Kim
thought about himself: "I am a Son of the Charm—I,
Kim." [13] Then, he suddenly asked himself: "Who is Kim-
Kim-Kim?" [14] Along with the Hindu *bairagi*, he went to
Benares where he met the lama. He also met a Jat whose
son was sick, and he gave him six lozenges which cured the
child. The lama showed Kim a sheet of scented China paper
on which was drawn the picture of the Wheel of Life with
its six spokes—the six evils and temptations. He wished to
take to the road again because, the lama said, he would not
find the River without Kim's aid. The Jat accompanied them
on the *te-rain* where they met an unhappy Maharatta, who
turned out to be also part of the game, E.23 of the Secret
Service. Kim helped the Mahratta, disguising him with the
outfit of the Jat by smearing ash on his bosom. Kim used
the skills he learnt at Lurgan's shop in order to save the
Mahratta from disaster. The Mahratta disappeared, and Kim
and the lama reached Delhi.

In chapter 12 the secret agent E.23, disguised by Kim,
left the train at Delhi and passed on a secret message covered
by a great many curses. Then, Kim and the lama detrained
at Saharunpore and wandered off into the countryside instead of going to the Kulu woman's house. The lama asked
Kim not to exercise charms, upon which Kim demanded to
know whether "all doing is evil." The lama answered that
"to abstain from action" is good, except when a person
tried "to acquire merit." Kim then replied that he was told
that "to abstain from action was unbefitting a Sahib" and

that he was a Sahib. The lama and Kim met Hurree Chunder Mookerjee, who was disguised as a professional physician. The Babu told them of his experiences in the Game, the situation of the Five Kings, and his plans to visit Mussoorie and meet the enemy spies who were already at work in the area. The lama liked the suggestion of travel in the cool hills. He believed he was instrumental in making the prophecy about Kim's meeting the Red Bull on a green field come true, and now, he said to Kim. "Thou shalt find me my River, being in return the instrument. The Search is great."

Chapter 13 tells of the lama's visit to and experience in the hills, which exemplify the belief that he "who goes to the Hills goes to his mother." Kim and the lama crossed deeper into the mountain ranges and each day "Kim watched the lama return to a man's strength." The lama proudly declared: "This is *my* country," but Kim, who was after all a man of the plains, could not feel much comfort in walking the narrow mountain paths. Both the lama and Kim meditated upon the Wheel of Life since they were away from at least its visible temptations. They met a Frenchman and a Russian who were coming from Leh in northern Kashmir and had a general letter of introduction. Hurree Chunder Mookerjee helped them with the problem of finding coolies and also answered their questions. They gave him gin and, consequently, Hurree became garrulous, babbling tales of oppression, shedding tears, grumbling about his low salary, and, finally, he staggered away singing Bengali love songs. The Russian said that Hurree represented "India in transition — the monstrous hybridism of East and West." The lama began to explain the Wheel of Life which he had drawn on paper, and the Russian "snatched half-jestingly at the chart which tore in lama's grip." The lama was shocked by this insult, and before Kim could intervene the Russian struck the holy man full on the face. The Frenchman fumbled with his revolver, but the coolies took hold of the "baggage" containing the papers in the *kilta* with the red top and fled up the hill. The Frenchman fired after them. Kim was furious, and he tried to pull the trigger of his gun. The lama successfully dissuaded Kim from shooting in return. Shooting ceased, and Kim and the lama, both unhurt, decided to go with the coolies to Shamlegh-under-the Snow. They poured a little liquor in the lama's mouth as medicine and he recovered his strength quickly. Kim and Hurree procured the *kilta* from the coolies since it contained important papers concerning the Game and eight months' good diplomatic work.

In chapter 14 the lama meditates near Shamlegh on this incident and its relation to good and evil, reality and illusion in the context of the meaning of the Wheel. He thought the blow struck by the Russian "was but a shadow upon a shadow," and that it was necessary for him to be rid of all passion. Kim thought the reasoning was "too high" for him, and the lama began to inquire into "the Cause of Things." A fair-skinned woman with turquoise-studded headgear appeared before Kim and watched him with bold, bright eyes. She made overtures to him, saying that she was "no common bearer of babes." Though he did not reciprocate, he persuaded her to carry a message to Hurree Babu. Hurree Babu in accordance with this message followed the spies in the area. Though the woman came back, she and Kim eventually had to part. Their parting scene is touching. Kim held out his hand, Western style, and she grasped it mechanically, "Good-bye, my dear." "Good-bye, and—and"—the woman was trying to recollect her English ". . . Good-bye, and—thee God bless you."

In chapter 15 Hurree Babu displays his resourcefulness in conducting the Russian and the Frenchman to Mashobra tunnel and in piloting them to Alliance Bank at Simla. They presented him with a certificate praising his "unerring skill as a guide." In the Doon valley lay the sick lama who was still searching for the River which would heal him. He thought the great arrow fell somewhere near the plains. Kim nursed the lama with great devotion and rubbed the holy man's feet. The lama said appreciatively, "Never was such a *chela*.[15] I doubt at times whether Ananda [16] more faithfully nursed our Lord. And thou art a Sahib? . . . It is strange." Kim, overwhelmed by the lama's affection, said he was "neither a Sahib nor an alien" and that there was "neither black nor white." The two set out again on their search for the River. Although they walked only half a *kos* on the ground, the lama covered thousands of miles in the world of the spirit. Kim sent a message to the Kulu woman about the Lama's declining health. The lama told Kim that there were many lies and liars in the world, "but there are no liars like our bodies," and yet Kim devoutly kissed the lama's feet. The woman of Kulu looked after them and fed them. Hurree appeared as a physician and told Kim of the happenings in Simla. Kim was told that Mahbub Ali was in the area selling horses and Hurree was to catch a train for Umballa: "What a beast of wonder is a Babu!" Kim was unwell and his thoughts were centered on the lama and their relationship: "I like Kim. I am Kim; and what is Kim?" He was about to lose his poise but it was restored to him by the "Mother Earth." In the evening Kim, squatting by the white wall, saw the lama and Mahbub Ali come to him. "What a fool's trick to play in open country!" muttered Mahbub. The lama paid Kim high compliments: "never was such a *chela*." They talked about the bond between them and realized that they were "at the end of the pilgrimage." The lama fell by a stream and believed he had found the River through his knowledge, and that Kim had aided him in the search. The lama declared that the search was finished and that in the process the soul detached itself from the body and became free. Kim and the lama both thought it was a marvel indeed. The holy man believed that the River of the Arrow was at his feet, that he had found it and, consequently, he was free and sinless, attaining salvation.

In offering this elaborate summary of the narrative content of *Kim*, I am aware that it is bound to falsify the intricate structural and thematic pattern of the novel. But such a procedure is useful in this case because *Kim* is so discursive and sprawling that at first sight one is apt to overlook the continuity of its theme. Moreover, the summary is useful not only in indicating the novel's thematic unity, but also in providing the basic frame on which to build my own argument.

The basic concern of the novel, as has been already suggested, is to indicate the different phases of Kim's growth to complete selfhood. This is, as it were, a transition from Kim's consciousness of himself as a Sahib among aliens, in the beginning of the novel, to that of "a true *chela*" of the holy lama, a modern "Ananda who kisses the lama's feet" at the end. Kim tells the lama, "perhaps, I was once a Sahib," and the holy man responds with great feeling, "was never a Sahib like thee, I swear it." It is in tracing this process of Becoming that *Kim* attains its central meaning and significance.

Since the main intention is to chart the process of inner growth, *Kim* cannot be judged or construed as an ordinary novel of chronological narration and description. Its thematic implications demand a different kind of structure. Basically there is a tension between Kim's suspected loss of identity and the assumed sense of selfhood. On the other hand, Kim feels himself to be an alien among natives, and on the other, he experiences a compulsive, though vague, urge to identify himself with the bustling Indian life. Thus he alternates between the threatened loss of identity among aliens and the sense of individuality stemming, surprisingly enough, from his sneaking affection for India. Kipling's main problem in *Kim* was to depict this dichotomy. This could be done only by means of pervasive symbol and imagery which make *Kim* not so much a novel as, to use F. R. Leavis's phrase, "a dramatic poem." The narrative sequence of the novel, as a result, is endowed with a profound significance emerging from several clearly discernible, though highly suggestive major symbols.

Among the symbols which are central to the dramatic structure of *Kim*, the River, the Road, and the Wheel stand out as the most significant. Together they contribute to the principal rhythm of the novel. The Grand Trunk Road sweeps across the great Indian peninsula encompassing in its variegated texture the rich, pulsating life of the Indian people. It represents not merely the journey of Kim's life but also his life-style. He grows, in fact, in and around the road as the poorest of the poor whites. When he suddenly disappears from St. Xavier's, he justifies this by saying that he must be permitted to take to the road for the period of vacations. Kim's activities hinge on the road—he procures rice and curry from the shop of a *kunjri*, subdues the Brahminee bull, begs for the lama, accompanies him on his journey by *te-rain*, drinks water native-fashion from the *bhisti*—all his actions demonstrate his close association and involvement with the road. The road, therefore, becomes a symbol of his Becoming—from childhood to manhood. He asks the water-carrier, "Give water here. We men are thirsty. "We men!" [17] said the *bhisti* laughing. Kim's use of the word "men" for the lama and himself suggests his awareness of growth even though to the *bhisti* he was a boy. The road provides the constantly changing stage of the drama of Kim's life. Mahbub Ali reports about Kim that "He had been out with Hurree on the road ere now" The drama of "the Game," of Lurgan Sahib and his shop, arises out of Kim's taking to the road. The road, in fact, seems to be a connecting link between many dramatic episodes in the novel.

Before analyzing the full implications of the Road as a symbol, one has to note some of the minor, but nevertheless highly suggestive, images used by Kipling in the course of the narrative. To begin with, the image of the horse or of "the white stallion" is linked up with the process of Kim's induction into the Great Game. The message carried by Kim to Creighton at Umballa refers to this: "The pedigree of the white stallion is fully established." It is obvious that broadly the image of the white stallion suggests the energy and vitality of British power in India. But Kim himself, at a later stage, is referred to as a pony in the Great Game who needs greater knowledge and experience of the world. Similarly, while the old soldier, Ressaldar Sahib, compares himself with "an old tortoise, . . . who puts his head out from the bank and draws it in again," [18] Kim associates himself with "a Red Bull on a green field." The images of the horse, mare, stallion, and pony form a pattern which is linked up with the image of the Red Bull on a green field. In this way the pattern of images in the novel is related to the process of Kim's experience. In fact this combination indirectly explains the links in his name: he is called *Kim Rishti ke* meaning Kim of the (Irish) Regiment. Kim, as it were, embodies the energy and beauty of the stallion as well as that of the Red Bull on a green field.

It is interesting to recall, in this context, another reference to the color red which is used often in *Kim* as a symbol of evil and falsehood. The lama makes this clear in the course of a conversation with Kim when he tells him: "I can see now that the sign of the Red Bull was a sign for me as well as for thee. All desire is red—and evil." Similarly, when the lama visits Kim again, compelled by his affection for the boy, he tells him: "I came . . . to see thee—misguided by the red mist of affection." [19] For the lama, it is clear, the color red denotes the falsity of earthly affection. It stands for untruth and unreality, and conversely white stands for purity and holiness. In the context of Kipling's alleged imperialistic stance, and the officially accepted red of the British Government in India, this gains a more meaningful association.

Similarly, Kim's journey on the Grand Trunk Road is suggested by the image of the bird. Used in relation to Kim it signifies his flights of fancy and the operative process of his imagination. Kim is described as "a most amazing young bird," in charge of "a yellow-headed buck-Brahmin priest." Kim's journey through the hills and on the extensive road is only the physical counterpart of his flights of fancy, and the significance of the bird image highlights the many varieties of his experience.

The lama's wanderings and visits to the sacred places in India, similarly, are symbolized by the turnstile in front of the museum. The turnstile suggests a circular movement which is exemplified by the lama's repeated visits to Benares and other holy places. The Greco-Buddhist sculptures, fragments of statues from the Buddhist *stupas* [20] and *viharas* [21] also suggest the circular movement of the seekers of the spirit in terms of the Great Wheel. The wheel of things, which is circular, is only a religious and abstract counterpoint of the mechanical and material circular turnstile. The turnstile also suggests the movement and the rhythm of the lama's quest and Kim's search so picturesquely presented in their travels.

All the major symbols in the novel, however, are oriented toward illumining the process of Kim's growth, his Becoming, from the position of an "imp" to that of an "adult," from child to man. This process of Kim's attaining the full stature of his selfhood is influenced by three distinct but divergent forces embodied in the personalities of Mahbub Ali, the lama, and Father Victor. Mahbub was registered in the Indian Survey Department as C.25.IB. He takes the boy under his wing between his tenth and thirteenth year. He becomes Kim's mentor in acquiring practical knowledge of the world. The meeting between Kim and Mahbub at the Umballa racecourse amply demonstrates the Pathan's role in Kim's growth to manhood. It is Mahbub who persuades Kim to stay with Father Victor and learn rather than run away with the horse-dealer. Mahbub tells him:

> But, Little Friend of all the World, there is *my* honour and reputation to be considered. All the officer Sahibs in all the regiments and all Umballa, know Mahbub Ali. Men saw me pick thee up and chastise that boy . . . Be patient. Once a Sahib, always a Sahib. When thou art a man—who knows—thou wilt be grateful to Mahbub Ali.[22]

Mahbub's words show that he was himself aware of the crucial role he played in Kim's growth, from boyhood to manhood, from being a pony to being a white stallion.

The second force at work in molding Kim's career is the British power in both its secular and its religious aspects, represented partly in the figure of Father Victor. He suggests the religious authority of the British Establishment in India, whereas Mavericks and Creighton stand for the secular. Father Victor desires to reclaim what he regards as Kim's lost soul and tells him, "We'll make a man of you at Sanawar—even at the price o' making you a Protestant." But Kim's impish nature can hardly tolerate any confinement and he longs to escape. Here again Mahbub Ali's influence is crucial. He enables Kim to escape, and he tells Kim clearly that he wants to make a man of him: "Children should not see a carpet on the loom till the pattern is made plain. Believe me, Friend of all the World, I do thee great service.

. . . They will not make a soldier of thee." [23] The imagery is highly significant for it suggests that the carpet of Kim's boyhood is woven on the loom of experience by the weaver Mahbub Ali.

Thus Mahbub Ali is Kim's secular *guru*, initiating him into the art of life—of dealing with men and things. He exercises a decisive influence in perfecting Kim in several worldly activities, including spying, carrying secret messages, and performing other intricate tasks connected with the Game. Even in matters of sex his influence is felt by Kim. Mahbub, we are told, visits the house of dancing girls and Kim himself, we find, "had passed the time of day with one or two frivolous ladies at upper windows in a certain street, and naturally, in the exchange of compliments, had acquitted himself well." [24]

The process of Kim's Becoming, thus finds its apex under Mahbub's dynamic stewardship. Kim wore a red turban in Hindu style, which was changed to blue by Mahbub Ali, and Kim "stood up, externally at least, a Mohemmedan." Kim had disguised himself and interviewed a girl in the bazaar. He left Lucknow in native garb and traveled to Bombay and Karachi, eating Haj dinners. He also recited the Koran with the fine cadence of a Muslim priest. In Mahbub's company Kim began to feel "mechanically for the moustache that was just beginning," thereby indicating a naturally felt tension between his instinctive growth and the impact of Mahbub Ali on his boylike sensibility. Kim could easily assume another identity, for a specific purpose. He "found it easier to slip into Hindu or Mohammedan garb when engaged in certain businesses." [25] He had also worn "a complete suit of Hindu Kit," the "costume of a low-caste street boy," which he often used in yelling at festive crowds or in frolic on the river bank. Lurgan Sahib had dressed Kim in various garbs, as a young Mohemmedan noble, as an Oudh landholder in resplendent dress, and Kim responded admirably. He sang with joy as he changed dresses and changed speech and gesture accordingly. Kim attempted to play the role of a fakir begging doles at the roadside, and demonstrated the different sorts of language he would use to an Englishman, a Punjabi, or to a woman not wearing a *Khurta* veil. Kim's marvelous performance, which delighted Lurgan Sahib, is a dramatic portrayal of his process of becoming someone else.[26]

Kim's delicate character and sensibility are shaped by the dual impact of the lama and Mahbub Ali, though the former exercises a more powerful and enduring influence. The secular aspect of Kim's being, as already suggested, grows in association with Mahbub Ali, whereas the spiritual aspect blossoms in the company of the lama. In this way these two, between them, are responsible for the spiritual and physical maturity of Kim. But the most crucial influence in molding Kim's personality is that of the lama.

The lama and Kim feel a strong, though strange, undercurrent of mutual affection and regard from the very beginning. In an intensely moving scene, the lama calls Kim "O Friend of all the World!" Moreover, there is something childlike in the character of the lama and, as Kipling says, he was "simply as a child bewildered in a strange bed." His affection for Kim is something which transcends all rational explanations. He had known many men and could claim quite a few as disciples. But, as he himself tells Kim, "to none among men, if so be thou art woman-born, has my heart gone out as it has to thee—thoughtful, wise, and courteous; but something of a small imp." This impish quality, however, is only a passing phase in Kim's growth and it is the lama himself who acts as a powerful force in making Kim transcend this stage.

The lama and Kim develop, from the beginning, a deep mutual attachment. The scene of their parting on the eve of Kim's schooling, full of love and sorrow, gives us a clue to this relationship. Lama looks upon Kim as a kindred soul hankering after freedom—after, so to say, realization of complete selfhood. This makes the lama dissuade Kim from becoming a soldier. Alluding to the sterility of secular life, the lama tells Kim: "These men follow desire and come to emptiness. Thou must not be their sort." Kim, for his part, completely surrenders himself to the lama, telling him unequivocally, "I am thy *chela*," and this intense loyalty makes the lama himself wonder whether the boy was "a spirit, sometimes, or sometimes an evil imp." Kim declares that "except for Mahbub Ali, and he is a Pathan, I have no friend, save thee, Holy One." Similarly, when the lama was attacked by the Russian, Kim valiantly protects his *guru*. Mahbub Ali himself entrusts Kim to the lama requesting him to guide "the colt" in the future.

This curious relationship between the lama and Kim gives us a clue to the significance of the major symbols of the novel, the Road, the River, and the Way. The lama bows before the Excellent Law of the Buddha and confesses to the curator his desire to attain freedom from the Wheel of Life. With touching humility he tells him: "I know nothing —nothing do I know—but I go to free myself from the Wheel of Things by a most broad and open road." The lama's abstract and spiritual conception of the road is juxtaposed with Kim's conception of it as "a wonderful spectacle," and the old soldier's assertion ". . . the great road which is the backbone of all Hind." Kim's road and the lama's way may be taken as the concrete and the abstract aspects of one indivisible, relentless pursuit. The lama's following a way is paralleled with and concretized by Kim's taking to the road. This suggests, broadly, Kipling's vision of the wholeness and unity of human experience in which the body and the soul, the real and the ideal, the here and the hereafter are delicately synthesized. The integrated image of the Road and the Way is the novelist's means of achieving this synthesis. Thus the elements of abstractions and those of concretions are seen in a continual process of harmonization in *Kim*.

The Road and the Way, however, are not the only images which attain a peculiar dimension of significance from the character of the lama. There is the major symbol of the River. Obviously, whereas the Road is an image of stability and solidity, the River is a symbol of flux, of rapid movement and change. Kipling himself was conscious of the majestic significance of the river which he describes as "a river of life which exists nowhere else in the world." Therefore, the River is no ordinary stream, and it is indeed the river of healing, because, it rose from the point where the Buddha's arrow—Moses-like—touched the earth and the waters gushed forth. It is the fountain of wisdom and whoever is able to reach it attains salvation. As the lama himself tells it: "My *chela* aided me to the River. It is his right to be cleansed from sin—with me." But the significance of the River which forms the central symbol cannot be explicated completely unless it is placed in the wider philosophic context of Buddhism and its counterpart, Lamaism.

It is clear that, next to Kim, the lama occupies a very vital place in the design of the novel. It is the lama who embodies the ideas and tenets of Buddhism as practiced in Tibet and, therefore, John Munro's comment that "Kim's progress through the novel parallels that of Buddha" is only partially true. Lamaism is a Tibetan variation of Buddhism, though it is partly derived from Tibet's ancient faith Bon-Po. It is also linked with the Tantric versions of Buddhistic faith. The central concept of Buddhism, as enunciated by Gautama, the Buddha, is the gospel of universal salvation based on belief in the unity and oneness of all beings. It believes that existences, admittedly, are manifold, but they are only manifestations of the essential unity which is a fundamental quality of life.

In the Buddhist view of the world different forms of existence, known as *Dhatu*, are only abodes of the minds of men and beings. Each possessor of mind gets a form and a place in accordance with his merits. There are six forms of existence to be attained through a progression or current, known as *Gati*, from a state of suffering to a state of joy. Three lower forms, the lowest being Hell, constitute the stage of suffering, whereas the other three higher forms comprise the stage of joy. Transmigration from one stage to another, or from one tabernacle to another, is denoted by death followed by rebirth, thus leading to the unceasing cycle of life-death-rebirth. *The Nirvana* or the Path of Duty is the true way to salvation from this continuous cycle of life and death, and a true seeker of the spirit can attain this deliverance from the pain of being born again and again in an endless chain of living. Thus, one of the cardinal principles of Buddhism is that of cause and effect. Our desires and attachments are the causes of our misery and pain. Moreover, the area in which this theory of causation operates is very wide in Buddhist cosmology. Therefore, a single action in the present is the result of the impact of innumerable causes in the past. Our actions lead to several reactions, and the sum total of human life is a natural corollary of our doings. But the aim of human life is to dissociate oneself from this long chain of cause and effect—in short, to attain *Nirvana*.

It is to remind humanity of this and to show the Way once again that Gautama, the Buddha, appeared. Buddhism believes that several religious prophets have appeared in antiquity, but Sakya Muni or Gautama is the Buddha for this age. Several Buddhas preceded him but Sakya Muni has shown the Way to the prevailing phase of humanity. Therefore, although the Buddha has revealed the Eternal Law to all men, this Law was in existence even before Buddha. Like Shaw's Life Force or Bergson's *elan vital*, for instance, the Law has existed independently of any person who might have realized it for himself. The Law is eternal and immutable and the Buddha is great because he once again made humanity aware of its existence. As the Buddha himself declared:

> *To give rest to every creature,*
> *I appear in the world,*
> *And, to the hosts of the living,*
> *Preach the pure Law, Sweet as dew;*
> *The one and only Law*
> *Of Deliverance and Nirvana*
> *With one transcendent voice*
> *I proclaim this truth,*
> *Ever taking the Great vehicle*
> *As my subject.*[27]

This belief in the recurring appearance of the Buddha to show the way to *Nirvana* suggests another basic Buddhistic doctrine which has crucial implications so far as the character of the lama in *Kim* is concerned. Buddhism—and its Tibetan variation, Lamaism—holds that the deliverance of a few individual beings is not enough and that what is needed is the salvation of entire humanity. Unless this is achieved individual spiritual emancipation will remain incomplete and imperfect. It is in this context of the basic Buddhist belief in universal salvation that the lama thinks of Kim as being cleansed from all sin by virtue of his help in the search for the River. Similarly, the lama exhorts even Mahbub Ali to follow the Way: "Why not follow the Way thyself and so accompany the boy?" Mahbub is not able to understand the rationale behind this exhortation. He does not know that the lama believes, as all Buddhists do, that individual salvation is imperfect until it encompasses all. As John Greenleaf Whittier (1807–92) has effectively expressed it in his poem "The Meeting": "He findeth not who seeks his own/The Soul lost that's alone."

But the Buddhist doctrine itself is divided into two systems with regard to the modes of salvation. In the *Hinayana* [28] the individual saves himself whereas in the *Mahayana* [29] the mind-possessor helps kindred souls, along with his own, to seek deliverance from the cycle of life. The *Mahayana* Buddhists look upon their Master as the living, loving, Embodiment of Enlightenment (Bodhi) and self-denial. It is His renunciation of all princely pleasures in *Kapilavastu* that makes a great impact on their sensibility. His great self-sacrifice and devoted adherence to the principle of spiritual freedom for all men seem to them His great qualities. It is thus the spirtiual, the personal, the esoteric, as well as the aesthetic aspects of Buddhism which are emphasized in the *Mahayana* doctrines (also in the lama's exhortations in *Kim*), which are expounded at length in the *Surangam Sutra* and the *Diamond Sutra*.

But the character of the lama has another dimension of significance since the Tibetan Lamaism is related to and closely derives from the Tantric school of Buddhism.[30] This emphasizes the esoteric mode of realizing the Divine. This includes processes of what Agehananda Bharati has called "psycho-experimental speculation," [31] as well as mystical or occult modes of gaining knowledge. It is against this background of Buddhism—and its Tibetan variation called

Lamaism—that the full significance of the lama in *Kim* emerges. Kipling's references to "Ananda's Lord—the Bod-hisat," [32] and the lama's ecstasy in contemplating the statue of the Great Sakya Muni are particularly significant in this context. Moreover, the lama's affection and solicitude toward Kim are perfectly in tune with the basic Buddhistic belief of universal salvation. A Bodhisattva, or an enlightened soul, achieves salvation for himself, but he is also animated by the desire to bring deliverance for all. Therefore, he refuses to enter the state of bliss or *Nirvana*,[33] inspired by the ideal of universal bliss. The lama's attitude to Kim is obviously an extension of this fundamental tenet of Buddhism.

From this perspective the closing scene of the novel is the apex of philosophical and mystical contemplation. Here the lama describes to Kim how he experienced the reward of his search for the River, how he meditated for two days without food, and how he realized the wise soul releasing itself from the silly body experiencing the bliss of *Nirvana*:

Yea, my soul went free, and, wheeling like an eagle, saw indeed that there was no Teshoo Lama nor any other soul. As a drop falls into water, so my soul drew near to the Great Soul which is beyond all things. At that point, exalted in contemplation, I saw all Hind, from Ceylon in the sea to the Hills, and my own painted rocks at Suchzen; I saw every camp and village, to the least, where we have ever rested. I saw them at one time and in one place; for they were within my soul. By this I knew the soul had passed beyond the illusion of Time and Space and of Things. By this I knew that I was free. I saw thee lying in thy cot, and I saw thee falling down hill under the idolater—at one time, in one place, in my soul, which, as I say, had touched the Great Soul. Also I saw the stupid body of Teshoo Lama lying down, and the *hakim* from Dacca kneeled beside, shouting in its ear. Then my soul was all alone, and I saw nothing, for I was all things, having reached the Great Soul. And I meditated a thousand years, passionless, well aware of the Causes of all Things. Then a voice cried: "What shall come to the boy if thou art dead?" and I was shaken back and forth in myself with pity for thee; and I said: "I will return to my *chela* lest he miss the Way." Upon this my soul, which is the soul of Teshoo Lama, withdrew itself from the Great Soul with strivings and yearnings and retchings and agonies not to be told. As the egg from the fish, as the fish from the water, as the water from the cloud, as the cloud from the thick air; so put forth, so leaped out, so drew away, so fumed up the soul of Teshoo Lama from the Great Soul. Then a voice cried: "The River! Take heed to the River!" and I looked down upon all the world, which was as I have seen it before—one in time, one in place—and I said: "Yonder is the River of the Arrow at my feet." At that hour my soul was hampered by some evil or other whereof I was not wholly cleansed, and it lay upon my arms and coiled round my waist; but I put it aside, and I cast forth as an eagle in my flight for the very place of the River. I pushed aside world upon world for thy sake. I saw the River below me—the river of the Arrow —and, descending, the waters of it closed over me; and behold I was again in the body of Teshoo Lama, but free from sin, and the *hakim* from Dacca bore up my head in the waters of the River. It is here! It is behind the mango-tope here—even here! [34]

In this climactic scene the lama is not merely dramatizing the esoteric and aesthetic elements of Tibetan Buddhism, an offshoot of the *Mahayana* school, but weaving the philosophy of his life into the delicate fabric of his inwardly-realized relationship with Kim. He is keen on seeing Kim as much cleansed from sin as he is himself because the boy is his dear *chela* who aided him in his search for the River of the Arrow. The tension caused by the lama's inability to find the River is finally resolved in this dramatic scene and the River is no longer an intangible myth, but a tangible reality. It is a revelation of immanence, that God is within us and not without. So is the River flowing at the lama's feet as a tangible, inwardly-realized reality.

Yet Kim himself remains torn between his attraction for

the lama and his fascination for Mahbub Ali. It is this dichotomy which leads him to question, in a moment of rare
self-introspection, his own identity: "I am Kim. I am Kim;
and what is Kim?" This self-questioning arises out of the
tension in his consciousness created by the contrary influ-
ences at work. He is attracted to the earthly, practical mode
of action generated by Mahbub Ali and he is also deeply affected by the other-worldly, ideal, spiritual mode of contemplation revealed by the lama. These two contraries, operating
in his consciousness, create the tension which makes him
question, in moments of abstraction, his own selfhood. Although Kim would not entirely resolve the dilemma between
these two opposite forces, yet he appeared to assume the
position of the lama's *chela*. Emotionally and spiritually he
is involved with the lama's River, yet he is not dissociated
from the Grand Trunk Road. Ultimately in a final attempt
at a synthesis of these contraries, he realizes that the Road is
a River of Men moving to their destiny and that the Road
and the River are only the two aspects of one, single, indivisible reality.

4

Minor Fiction

It has been said that Kipling wrote novels merely to discover that he could not become a competent and successful novelist, and that therefore he turned more and more to the short story, which proved to be an apt choice. The falsity of this view has been amply demonstrated by *Kim*, Kipling's masterpiece. The hollowness of this view is further confirmed by Kipling's two excellent novelettes, *Captains Courageous* and *The Light That Failed*.

This mistaken judgment about Kipling's achievement as a novelist is a natural consequence of the misreading of the nature of the novel as a genre. The novel is a mixed genre and its genesis can be traced to several other forms such as romance, biography, essay, and drama. Since the novel is a comparatively new form making a real start as late as the eighteenth century, it has very little of traditional aesthetic. However, in the twentieth century the criticism of the novel has grown tremendously as compared with the criticism of the other genres. Those critics who take a rather narrow and selective view of the form of the novel may not even consider *Kim* or *Captains Courageous* as real novels and their quarrel with Kipling will be primarily about the purity and homogeneity of the form. I feel that the purist's view of the form is misconceived and that Kipling as an artist registers remarkable success primarily because as a novelist he challenges the conventional criteria of the novel.

Captains Courageous is Kipling's very distinctive kind of fiction since it does not fit into the traditionally accepted norms of the novel. The narrative content is "so slight," writes J. M. S. Tompkins, that "it is little more than a way of organizing the descriptive substance."[1] Tompkins has very rightly raised the question of the novel's structure, which is not narrative in the conventional sense, but is primarily based on the evocation of the element of atmosphere and the exploration of the growth of human personality. Kipling is a genuine artist because his mode of communication is exceptionally exciting and gripping. The reader is carried away by the sweep and rapidity of the movement of the novel. Through his marvelous powers of observation, evocation, and description, Kipling breathes life into the scenes of fishing and makes the world of the sea come alive to the reader.

Kipling as an artist is aware of the true function of the novel, which lies in a genuine presentation of actuality, in the working of life into art. From this point of view, *Captains Courageous* is full of exciting action and the activist in Kipling finds full expression in it. In fact, like *Kim*, it shows the process of Kipling's growth, his transformation from activist into artist.

The problem of the representation of reality is not merely a matter of the mode of narration or description; it is essentially a matter of the artist's vision. The most significant aspect of *Captains Courageous* is the re-creation of the fisherman's world in the visionary cosmos of Kipling's all-pervasive imagination. The schooner *"We're Here"* is a world in herself; she is the miniature of a larger world; she is a world in microcosm. The reader gets insights into the fishermen's world, its exhausting and exciting routine, its daily risks and dangers, its joys and sorrows. This world of sailors and ships is brought into association with the world of finance and industry which gives rise to the dramatic tension in the novel. The facets of the fishermen's life are revealed and their points of contact with actuality are effectively presented.

The question whether the reality in *Captains Courageous* is rooted in the character or the situation has baffled many critics. Whereas Thomas R. Henn believes that *Captains Courageous* is the "story of the spoilt only child of an American millionaire" and "of a neurotic and charming mother," and that the "design of the book"[2] implies that the "character of Harvey Cheyne should mature" by conventional shocks, Mark Kinkead-Weekes thinks that "it is a book about fishing, not a story of 'personality.'"[3] In my view, it seems to be both, since man and nature are involved in an encounter and in the process of experience man is altered.

It is necessary to sum up briefly what the novel is about, so that the connection between its subject matter and its vision can be properly perceived. The spoiled, vain, pampered Harvey Cheyne is presented traveling with his parents on a steamer from New York to Europe. The copassengers think of this boy as "the biggest nuisance aboard," as he was "too fresh." A German passenger remarked "I know der breed. Ameriga is full of dot kind."[4] Aspects of the theme of the novel are introduced even on the first page of the first chapter. The New Yorker says that Harvey is "going to Europe to finish his education," while the Philadelphian comments, "Education isn't begun yet." The substance of *Captains Courageous* is primarily concerned with the processes of Harvey Cheyne's education, education for life and for understanding the complex art of living.

Harvey Cheyne was fainting from seasickness. His head swelled and his heels wavered in the air. He fell from the deserted deck into the sea and was rescued by Manuel, a member of the crew of the fishing schooner, *We're Here.* Earlier on the deck he tried to smoke a "real Turkish cig" and he pompously declared, "I'm an American—first, last, and all the time. I'll show 'em that when I strike Europe." He then found himself on a pile of half-dead fish in a dory. He met Dan and his father, Disco Troop, of Gloucester. He accused his rescuers of stealing his pocket money but soon realized his error. Harvey was called "young feller" by Disco and asked to do "menial work" which was the beginning of his education. Harvey then took Dan into confidence and told him about his father, a railroad financier, and his sentimental, neurotic mother. Harvey and Dan went fishing in Dan's dory and the story of the boy's learning the professional skill of the hard life of fishermen is narrated in eight chapters of the novel. He learnt the art of "roughing it," which is part of the American fable.

When Kipling in *Something of Myself* spoke of catching

and holding "Something of a rather beautiful localized American atmosphere," he probably implied this facet of the American experience. It is part of America's great pioneering tradition which has found expression in Thoreau, Whitman, Melville, Hemingway, and Faulkner. Kipling's close friendship with his family doctor, James Conland, who was a great weaver of yarns and a lover of fishing, was really instrumental in making him write *Captains Courageous* with exceptionally profound professional competence. In the novel, Harvey himself acquires this professional know-how and has become a much better young man when he meets his parents again in chapter 9. From this point of view, chapter 9 is the crucial part of the novel because it presents the scene of the meeting between Harvey and his parents at Albany. The plot becomes complex by the induction of subsidiary motives, the romance between Milsom, the secretary, and the typist, Miss Kinzey, and the peculiar meeting between Cheyne and Troop. Mrs. Cheyne says it is a wonder her son's "nervous system isn't completely wrecked." Harvey answered that he "worked like a horse" and "ate like a hog" and "slept like a dead man." Mrs. Cheyne wished to offer money as a reward to Manuel, which he at first refused. Pressed hard, he agreed to take five dollars and introduce her to the Portuguese priest to whom she made a generous contribution. Manuel took part in the blessings showered on Mrs. Cheyne for her charity. In the last chapter the novelist tells us that "Harvey was his father's shadow" and that for the first time Harvey began to realize his father's matter-of-fact approach to, and knowledge of, life. The father revealed to his son the moments of his life when he "hung on the ragged edge of despair," but held on to his faith—the "faith that comes of knowing men and things." [5] This story held Harvey almost breathless and it seemed to him as exciting as "watching a locomotive storming across country in the dark," and he gasped, saying, "It's just the greatest thing that ever was!"

Thus the world of *Captains Courageous* is a world of moral values, of invincible faith in activism as a way of life. Harvey's personality is transformed by his experience of the rugged life of Gloucester fishermen, and at the same time, he also realizes the worth of his father's varied and extensive experience. The two worlds meet in a single fount which sustains the vision of courageous captains.

Captains Courageous is completely rooted in reality yet it soars high in visionary gleam. The fact that the schooner *We're Here* makes constant contact with water, and sometimes with land, and always with air indicates her close touch with the actual and the real. Even the name of the schooner *We're Here* is significant, since it suggests the world here and now, the all pervasive and overpowering reality of the present and the palpable. The description of *Captains Courageous* as a brilliant documentary of the life of fishermen is not quite acceptable, yet one cannot overlook the exceptionally true-to-life account of the fishermen's life in it. Kipling's professional knowledge of this life is at its best in this novel of activistic creed. The description of the schooners in chapter 8 and the experience of Harvey is vivid and knowledgeable.

"The dories roved and fished and squabbled" until a swell came over the waters. If the swell continued, the Virgin, the rock twenty feet below the sea's surface, would go to pieces. The description of Long Jack rowing up in this situation is marvelous.

> "Can't ye hear ut knockin'?" he cried. "Pull for your miserable lives! Pull!"
>
> The men swore and tried to argue as the boat drifted; but the next swell checked a little, like a man tripping on a carpet. There was a deep sob and a gathering roar, and the Virgin flung up a couple of acres of foaming water, white, furious, and ghastly over the shoal sea. Then all the boats greatly applauded Long Jack, and the Galway men held their tongue.[6]

Kipling effectively conveys the excitement of the fishermen involved in this episode. *Captains Courageous* is built around such facets of experience, scenes, and events, which turn Kipling the activist, the exciting adventurer, into an enduring artist.

The Light that Failed (1890) is one of the most enigmatic creations of Kipling's art. This novel has had two versions, each with a different ending. It first appeared as a novelette telling a somber love story, portraying scenes of war, but with a rather contrived happy ending. A little later it reappeared in a larger volume with an equally contrived but tragic finale. Kipling in a one-sentence preface explained that "this is the story of *The Light that Failed* as it was originally conceived by the writer." He probably implied that his original vision was tragic and that that was implicit in the title.

The second revealing aspect of *The Light that Failed* is its close and intimate connection with certain events in Kipling's own life. Several critics have already noted the points of resemblance between Dick Heldar's and Maisie's childhood experiences and Kipling's own as recorded in *Something of Myself*, especially in respect to the "House of Desolation." Carrington has perceptively commented upon the similarities between Dick Heldar's experiences and those of Punch in "Baa, Baa, Black Sheep." Both these experiences could be related to Kipling's own experience as recorded in *Something of Myself*. He writes of the "House of Desolation": "It was an establishment run with the full vigour of the Evangelical as revealed to the Woman. I had never heard of Hell, so I was introduced to it in all its terrors." [7]

In "Baa Baa, Black Sheep" Aunty Rosa had introduced to Punch "an abstraction called God," the "intimate friend and ally" of the woman. And then, Punch learnt that the Lord was "the only thing in the world more awful than Aunty Rosa." [8] The spirit of this narration resembles greatly the way of Dick's feelings, described in the first chapter of *The Light that Failed*. Dick's responses to Mrs. Jennett are very similar to those of Kipling in relation to the "Woman":

> The many hours that she could spare from the ordering of her small house she devoted to what she called the home-training of Dick Heldar. Her religion, manufactured in the main by her own intelligence and a keen study of the Scriptures, was an aid to her in this matter. At such times as she herself was not personally displeased with Dick, she left him to understand that he had a heavy account to settle with his Creator; wherefore Dick learned

to loathe his God as intensely as he loathed Mrs. Jennett; and this is not a wholesome frame of mind for the young.[9]

The points of resemblance between Kipling's autobiographical commentary, the substance of the story "Baa Baa, Black Sheep," and the process of the growth of Dick and Maisie in *The Light that Failed* are too pervasive and overwhelming to be brushed aside by any intelligent observer. This biographical evidence has been adduced only to underscore the existence of a very lose relationship between Kipling's own life and that of Dick Heldar in the substance and structure of the story.

Kipling's own reminiscences as a struggling journalist in India, as pointed out by J. M. S. Tompkins, find expression "through the lips of" [10] Dick or Torpenhow or the Nilghai. The motif of inducting professional war correspondents or artists who draw sketches of battles is linked up with the novelist's intention to show the debasement of the practitioners of art in their pursuits. To Kipling art is pure and sacred, and it is also woven into the fabric of the novel's main theme.

The theme of *The Light that Failed* is basically life's fulfillment, though it touches, on a subsidiary level, several strands such as love, art, blindness, war, and an activistic creed. In my view, it is not a "war novel" although the war, or actions of war, loom large on its horizon. In a perceptive essay, "*The Light that Failed* as a war Novel," Eric Solomon has analyzed and interpreted its controlling cosmos. "Although not the subject" of the novel, he writes, "war becomes the controlling theme of *The Light that Failed*." [11] It is true because many events in the novel are directly or indirectly concerned with war and it also becomes a connecting link between the theme of action and the theme of art. Dick Heldar begins to draw sketches of war on his canvases. His blindness is caused by the wound inflicted in the war. And the atmosphere in the novel is dominated by war, or, as pointed out by C. F. G. Masterman by the idea of war.[12] Whether war comes in as an idea, or as an ugly, tangible reality it is obvious that war is one of the principal themes.

It is necessary to present a brief outline of the narrative content of *The Light that Failed* as a preparatory ground for critical analysis. Chapter 1 introduces Dick Heldar and Maisie as boarders in a seaside town in England, since their parents are in India. Their confrontation with Mrs. Jennett, who is a highly puritanical person and extremely overbearing and unkind in attitude, is the main theme at this stage. The children go to the beach to shoot with cheap revolver. The pistol thus becomes a symbol of their defiance, their growing age, and approaching adulthood. It foreshadows the theme of violence and cruelty connected with the war. Maisie asks Dick to become an artist and Dick answers, "I'll be an artist, and I'll do things." [13] Their confrontation with Mrs. Jennett is effectively portrayed since she became livid and "prophesied an immediate judgment of Providence." In chapter 2 Dick becomes a war correspondent and follows his co-worker and friend, Torpenhow in the Sudan campaign. Torpenhow tells Dick, "You'd better stick to me. . . . You must justify your choice." [14] Dick is found in a state of delirium calling for Maisie, after watching a battle on the Nile. " 'Behold a phenomenon; said Torpenhow, . . . 'Here is a man, presumably human, who mentions the name of one woman only. And I've seen a good deal of delirium, too.' " [15] Dick is wounded in the forehead. In chapter 3 Dick returns to London, and is found starving by Torpenhow, who asks him to move into his chambers near Charing Cross. Dick's hundred and forty-seven sketches were taken by a man who called himself the "head of the Central Southern Syndicate." Dick secures their release from the syndicate man. As an artist, Dick begins to achieve fame in London's art world. Chapter 4 carries forward the story of the exhibition of his sketches. He meets Maisie, now a grown-up woman, and his body "throbbed" as he watched her "pearl-white" face through the fog. Maisie tells him about paintings and Dick says "I paint a little myself.' " She leaves him abruptly to catch a bus and he returns to his chambers. Torpenhow says that Dick is as "mad as a hatter." Dick shouts at Nilghai: "Then tells him . . . 'Only the free are bond, and only the bond are free.' " This is one of the paradoxical statements of Kipling which throws light on his concept of duty and work. In chapter 5 Dick's attachment for Maisie is shown, though she doesn't wish to marry him, preferring to devote herself to painting. Dick is addressed by Torpenhow as "Well, madman, how d'you feel?" Dick tries to articulate his predicament, "Torp, there's too much ego in my cosmos." Dick's case was not that of a "Liver out of order," but of displacement of his soul: "I suppose it's my soul." Chapter 6 continues the story of Dick's meeting with Maisie, this time at a seaside resort. He meets a red-haired girl at Maisie's apartment, her roommate, who "announced that she would make a study of Dick's head." Later, in cleaning the floor of the red-haired girl's room, the charwoman finds "two, not to say three, kind of soap, which is yaller, an' mottled, an' disinfectink" and wishes to know which she should use. The red-haired girl shouts at her, then looks at her own reflection in the mirror and covers her face "as though she had shouted some shameful secret aloud." Meanwhile, Torpenhow and Nilghai wonder at Dick's goings-on with a girl, fearing that he might soon be a respectable married man and "ruin his work for ever." Torp exclaims, "Ho! ho! I'd give something to see Dick 'go wooing with the boys.'" This is an odd expression of another subsidiary theme in the novel—the love and attachment between man and man.

In chapter 7 Dick talks of his love for Maisie, but she is unresponsive. Dick tells her: "But you must learn to forgive a man when he's in love." When he finds her keen on her painting career, he asks her to "stick to your money." He throws a silver coin into the river, after the Hindu custom, to ward off all evil coming to Maisie. Chapter 8 brings the company of men together, Dick, Torpenhow, and the Nilghai, with their love of music, art, and wanderings. Chapter 9 develops the theme of art; Maisie neglecting Dick's suggestion about line-work and playing with the absurd notion for a "fancy head." Maisie and the red-haired girl plan to go to Paris to work with the idea of the head of the Melancolia. Dick, though skeptical of their ability, sees them off at Dover. Meanwhile, Dick finds that Torpenhow has sheltered Bessie—"Broke"—whom Dick considers a fit model for

Melancolia. Chapter 10 introduces the theme of blindness, the light that fails. Dick, with failing eyesight consults an oculist, whose diagnosis is not optimistic. Dick continues to paint the Melancolia, his best picture, and Torpenhow on a visit finds Dick a wreck. Chapter 11 presents Dick addicted to drink but still keen on his great picture. Torpenhow asks Dick to complete the picture within three days, but Bessie, now revengeful because Dick had interfered with her romance, destroys the picture. She loathed the picture because Torpenhow was taken in by it, and because he was completely ignoring her. Dick grows blind, raves and talks to Torpenhow of his deep love for Maisie. Chapter 12 dwells on the possibilities of war. Torpenhow goes to France to tell Maisie about Dick's misery. Chapter 13 narrates the story of Maisie and the red-haired girl in France, their plan for the head was not faring well, and Maisie is shocked to hear of Dick's horrible misfortune. Kipling introduces an element of surprise in the plot sequence by revealing that the red-haired girl was in love with Dick. In Chapter 14 Dick is taken out for a walk by his housekeeper. He meets Bessie and she confesses how she ruined the Melancolia. Then, Dick is taken to the bank and a passage to Port Said is booked. He makes his will, and prepares his kit for the journey. In chapter 15 Dick says good-bye to Bessie on the boat, and feels happy to be on board the steamer: "Oh, it's good to be alive again!" On arrival, his doctor takes him to Madam Binat's who receives him warmly: "The war is good for trade, my friend; but. . . ." Dick told her that in England he became blind, yet he "was too anxious to get to the front once more." Then, he goes to Suakin in a boat to meet his friend. "Thy friend! Chtt! Thy friend is death, then!" He hires a camel to join the British troop column and at the front in the face of enemy fire he really meets with his "friend"—death. Dick is shot and surrenders to "the crowning mercy of a kindly bullet through his head." He falls into the arms of Torpenhow.

This summary of events, however sketchy, is intended to convey the complex nature of the novel's structure and its multiple themes. The structure, as described by Thomas R.

Henn, is "episodic," and it is full of violence mollified by love. Yet, I do not agree with Henn's view that it is a "bad, but interesting novel" and that it has a "negative importance" [16] in Kipling's development as an artist. A novel could not be bad and interesting at the same time, particularly if the connotation of what is interesting is vague. In my view, Kipling is endeavoring to express in *The Light that Failed* an inwardly realized experience and the facets of that experience—love between man and woman, love between man and man, love of art, love of action and war—are central to Kipling's creative cosmos.

The Light that Failed has an intricate design, "it is full of echoes and correspondences" which have been analyzed by Miss Tompkins most admirably. Her contention that "emotion rises from inadequate causes" is true of the Dick-Maisie and Dick-Bessie relationships, and Kipling lapses into sentimentality in portraying Bessie's destructive passion as well as her later benevolence. Even the end, Dick courting his death in the desert, is too sentimental and contrived to achieve the dimension of a tragic finale.

Criticism of Kipling's cult of violence has been mounting over the years, though with different degrees of approaches. A hangover of the early short stories, this cult of violence, this love of cruelty and fighting is, to some extent, reflected in *The Light that Failed*. However, it seems to me more of an idea, a concept than a concrete factor. Max Beerbohm was shocked at what he thought was a wild demonstration of Kipling's involvement with war hysteria, and many others also expressed their revulsion at the alleged "cult of violence." This adverse criticism, in my view, seems out of focus with the reality of Kipling's basic sources of creativity. Criticism of the cult of cruelty and violence seems extremely one-sided, though one cannot cherish the scene of Dick Heldar glorying in the experience of soldiers shooting in the Sudanese campaigns.

However, it is the activism in Kipling that comes into full play in Dick Heldar's love of action and war. Then again, activism is also employed as a psychic means to overcome the frustration in love and art. Dick Heldar in his psychic

state approximates to the hero of Tennyson's *Maud* (1855).
Maud is a monodrama, since different phases of passion in
the hero take on the roles of different characters in the play.
The hero of *Maud* is angry, passionate, unbalanced, and when
frustrated in love he takes recourse to war and action. Dick
is not as much an introvert as Tennyson's hero is, but his
approach to the role of action and activism is similar. Dick
tries to escape from his world of frustration into a world of
desperate, thoughtless action, and from the world of action
into a universe of nothingness and death. *The Light that
Failed* thus demonstrates a phase of Kipling's art and life—
his transformation from the activist into the artist. It is a
little saga of his inwardly-felt experience turned into an enduring work of art.

5

Short Stories

Critical opinion has crystallized itself into acknowledging Kipling's greatness as a born storyteller with amazingly resourceful talent in handling a great variety of themes in this genre. In 1891 Andrew Lang welcomed Kipling as another Bret Harte, stating that his short stories have "the strangeness, the color, the variety, the perfume of the East."[1] Walter Pollock in a review of *Plain Tales from the Hills* in the *Saturday Review* praises Kipling as a "born story teller and a man of humour into the bargain."[2] Edmund Gosse, appreciating Kipling's skill in fiction, writes that his short stories are masterpieces of this genre and their place in English and European literature is very high. His stories possess masculine buoyancy, and that "power of sustaining an extremely spirited narrative in a tone appropriate to the action, which is one of Kipling's rare gifts."[3] Realism and creation of atmosphere are considered to be Kipling's great assets as a short-story writer. But he is equally a great artist in the fields of fantasy and fable. His short stories are an extraordinary synthesis of realism and lyricism. Chesterton's comment on the nature of Kipling's talents, that he is a "most extraordinary and bewildering genius,"[4] is particularly true of his short stories. Modern critics such as J. M. S. Tompkins[5] and C. A. Bodelsen[6] have offered very sensitive, profound, and intelligent insights into many of the short stories, yet the task is by no means complete.

A distinctive quality of Kipling as a short-story writer is the very wide range of his subject matter and the extraordi-

nary sweep of his imagination. His stories, like those on
Simla Hills, range from actuality of life, elements of experience of everyday life in India, England, the barrack-
room, the high seas, to exploration of the animal world and
also the world of fantasy exemplified in his immortal *Jungle
Books.* The range of his subject matter is shown in the many
themes of cruelty, violence, suffering, joys of masculine companionship, camaraderie, and feeling for a cause. Kipling is
primarily concerned with the real world, the world here and
now in all its beauty and beastliness, but he is also concerned
with the romantic and fabulous world, the world of the
hereafter. His stories revolving around ghosts or the idea of
reincarnation conjure up a fantastic universe which cannot
be described as real. The sweep of his imagination is so wide
that it extends over not only varieties of men but also lands
as far apart as England, Europe, Asia, and Africa, which become the living organisms of his art. The sweep is not merely
wide, it is also deep, and balanced by exploration in detail.
Kipling's stories reflect his insight into various layers of the
unconscious and the dimensions of the psyche which rise
in the structures of his tales. He is a genuine artist in exploring the wide variety of life in the form of his short
stories. It is of course true that the creative genius of Kipling
has to be considered a single, indivisible whole, and that his
roles as poet, novelist, short-story writer are only facets of
that one imaginative mind. Yet it must be said that it is in
the area of the short story that the best aspects of his creative
talent are vividly reflected.

It is not easy to explain adequately the real reasons behind
Kipling's immense popularity as a short-story writer nor is it
simple to formulate an appropriate mode of responding to
his work. He has had an ever-widening public who read him
with pleasure. Yet, at the same time, he was being underrated, particularly by academic critics. However, the adverse
tide underwent a change and the academics, too, began to
be less hostile to him. But their approach was different from
the ordinary reader's instinctive responses to Kipling's world.
The general reader read Kipling for the realistic portrayal
of varied segments of life, the color, the scenery, the charac-

ters, who, he thought, were endowed with verisimilitude. The academics offered elaborate analyses of theme and symbol, which were beyond the ken of an average reader. Thus, there seems to be a dichotomy between the scholar's and the ordinary reader's response to Kipling. However, the fascination for his work was commonly shared by both of them in their own special modes.

Verisimilitude is one of the outstanding qualities of Kipling's short stories and it has been acknowledged by new as well as old critics. He was the first short-story writer to create faithfully the scenes and atmosphere of the barrack-room and to make his soldiers seem real. His keen observation, his unflinching fidelity to the facts of life, and his innate power to create living, breathing, real people account for the deep impression of verisimilitude that he produces on the sensibility of his reader. Kipling is a professional of professionals, as is shown in his continuous search for finding the ways and methods of professionals. Examples of his interest in the work of professional artisans have been cited. On his walks Rudyard talked at length with builders, masons, carpenters, and craftsmen to know their skills, their lingo, their selective phraseology, their attitudes, and his comprehensive grasp of the day-to-day life of workmen is reflected in "The Bridge-Builders."

"Kipling," writes Randall Jarrell, "like it or not, admit it or not, was a great genius. . . . one of the most skillful writers who ever existed," who made the reader exclaim: "Well, I've got to admit it really is *written*." [7] This feeling, in my view, is the heart of the matter of Kipling's created world. Kipling cannot be described as a lord of language, a new Victorian Virgil, nor can he be considered one of the masters of English prose style. Yet it must be said that he used English with great skill and with telling effect. His use of Indian words or cockney speech gives a new vitality to his style. And, ultimately, the reader's response is beautifully summed up in these words: "Yes, it really is *written*. Really, it is, my word!"

"The Bridge-Builders" is one of Kipling's most fascinating stories not merely because its theme is so central to his philosophy of life but also because it attempts to bridge the gap between this world and the other, between reality and imagination, between prose and poetry. As the first story in *The Day's Work*, "The Bridge-Builders" sings the gospel of work, the doctrine of activism which is the cardinal element of Kipling's credo. The story is told on two levels— those of the physical and the spiritual—and the events in the story are passages to these. It is also a bridge between the human and the divine, this world and the other. The story is about the giant bridge over the Ganges "one mile and three-quarters in length, a lattice-girder" construction of great proportion supervised by Findlayson, the Chief Engineer of the Public Works Department. Kipling presents all the details of the physical reality with great accuracy and professional knowledgeability. Each of the twenty-seven piers of the bridge was twenty-four feet in diameter "capped with red Agra stone and sunk eighty feet below the shifting sand of the Ganges' bed." [8] Riveters swarmed about the lattices and the piers. The construction trains rattled and shrieked near the embankments pouring tons of white stone in the riverbed. Kipling paints a graphic scene of the pouring of the concrete that went into the making of the bridge. His presentation of the physical reality of the bridge, with all its materials, workmen, and the bustling life around the bridge, is vivid and living.

The physical reality of the bridge is closely linked with Findlayson's belief in activism as a value of living. He and his assistant Hitchcock had worked very hard for years through official red tape, the delays caused by the War, the cholera, the small-pox and other handicaps. Behind everything "rose the black frame of the Kashi Bridge—plate by plate, girder by girder, span by span—and each pier of it recalled Hitchcock." The bridge arose out of the initiative, calculations, and dedicated hard work of the two engineers.

Kipling swings to the human plane from the physical and we get a glimpse of bevies of workmen with their firepots and hammers working round the clock on the bridge. Then, there is Peroo, a skillful *Lascar* from Bulsar, who had traveled all over the world and gained wide experience, and who spoke wonderful English mixed with his lingo of Portugese origin. He was a genuine Hindu, deeply involved in the mysterious workings of the Hindu divinities. He asked Findlayson: "Our bridge is all but done. What think you Mother Gunga will say when the road runs over?" [9] Peroo had performed *poojah* in the big temple by the river for the God within, and he was the trusted lieutenant of Findlayson and Hitchcock.

Peroo's apparently casual remark about what Mother Gunga will think of the bridge being built across her sets into motion the bewildering forces of her swift currents. Telegrams are received warning the engineers of the rising floods of the Ganges and heavy rains, and Findlayson has only fifteen hours to save as much material as possible from the rising fury of the river. The night gongs and conches were sounded, and the naked, devoted workmen set to work in pale darkness clearing the riverbed and saving machinery and materials of all kinds. Findlayson was troubled by the stone-boats and the speed with which Mother Gunga had come bank-high, then he saw the big flood. He was calculating the relative strength of the piers and girders of the bridge, but who would know Mother Gunga's arithmetic! Peroo gave clear Malwa opium to the hungry Findlayson and both of them were swept away on a stone-boat by the swift current. They landed on an island several miles away. Findlayson was almost in a trancelike state and Peroo saw an assembly of gods, in animal shapes, on that mysterious island.

Kipling presents the second level—the spiritual—in this assembly on the island. In Hindu mythos animals are closely associated with gods. The stumps of the indigo plants crackled and a huge Brahminee bull made his appearance under a tree. Findlayson and Peroo both saw this vision before the shrine—the bull, the parrot, the blackbuck, a tigress —all came into their ken. Then the blunt-nosed Mugger (crocodile) of the Ganges draggled herself before the assembly. The crocodile complained that the waters of the Ganges were polluted and she was defiled. But the elephant answered the Gunga's charge that the bridge defiled her waters: "It is but the shifting of a little dirt. Let the dirt dig in the dirt if it pleases the dirt." [10] It is the vision of the eternal as against the temporal, the infinite against the finite, the immortal against the mortal. As Miss Tompkins, in her extremely perceptive analysis of "The Bridge-Builders" has pointed out, the "enormous bridge and its swarming life" [11] is reduced to an atom and the infinitesimal is displaced by the immeasurable.

The dimensions of the elements of the spirit in "The Bridge-Builders" are revealed through the Hindu Pantheon, or the assembly of gods, who discuss and give judgment on the complaints of the crocodile, which is the animalistic image of the Ganges. Shiv, Ganesh, Hanuman, and Krishna participate in the proceedings, and the final judgment is pronounced by Indra, the supreme god: "Ye know the Riddle of the Gods, when Brahm ceases to dream, the Heaven and Hell and Earth disappear. Be content. Brahm dreams still. The dreams come and go, and the nature of the dream changes, but still Brahm dreams." [12] Brahma created the universe in ecstasy and it rose out of his divine imagination. Indra says the divine dream continues and regeneration will follow decay and that the complaint of the Ganges regarding the bridge is like making disproportionate fuss over a little, transitory, dirt in a vast expanse. The mutable is silhouetted against the immutable, the transitory against the eternal. The material vastness of the bridge is thus reduced to infinitesimal smallness and the Hindu Pantheon is shown indirectly setting its seal on the project of the great bridge over the Gunga.

Kipling's vision connects the past with the present, and Hanuman, the Hindu god, as the leader of the "builders of the bridges as of old," is linked with the modern bridge-builders in British India. The continuity of human endeavor is suggested in this tradition from the past to the present, and this is similar to men's devotion to the gods. Shiv will be worshipped in schools, Ganesh shall have his worshippers, and people "will do no more than change the names" of the deities. The devotion will show the continuity of man's response. This continuity also marks the task of bridge-building by the ancients and the moderns, Hanuman and Findlayson. Kipling's visionary quality is revealed in the delicate poise which he creates between change and immutability, the temporal and the timeless. The poise points up the unity that he visualizes between past and present, between ancient and modern bridge-builders which is central to the theme of the story. "Yes, Findlayson's bridge was safe and serene," there's not a stone shifted anywhere, partly because it is a symbol of unity between the human and divine, past and present, temporal and eternal.

"The Miracle of Purun Bhagat," the first tale in *The Second Jungle Book*, is one of the most extraordinary stories of Rudyard Kipling. It is so superbly designed, tightly written, and dexterously controlled that the apparently sprawling flux of its material falls into shape, the shape of its vision. It seems to me a masterpiece of Kipling's art, partly because it demonstrates the basic process of his creativity. I have propounded, elsewhere in this book, the argument that Rudyard Kipling is essentially an activist in the late-Victorian tradition and that his activism is transformed into art in his fiction and poetry. "The Miracle of Purun Bhagat" demonstrates, in my view, this fundamental process operative in Kipling's creative mind of the transformation of the activist into artist. The story is, therefore, not merely Kipling's portrayal of Purun Bhagat, but also the creative writer's way of looking at his art.

Purun Dass was a man of action in his role as Prime Minister of one of the semiautonomous Indian princely states. He was a shrewd and diplomatic administrator since he knew how to please the two masters, the Indian Maharajah as well as the British Resident in the Indian State. This was "a difficult game," [13] but Purun Dass "played it coolly" and cleverly, and rose to the high office of the Prime Minister. He was very progressive in his outlook because he had had an English education at Bombay. He introduced several measures of reform and implemented a great many schemes of progress that the governments in his native state, Delhi, and London were delighted with. He became the honored friend of the Viceroy, the Governors, the Lieutenant-Governors, and hosts of others who formed the contemporary ruling Establishment. He produced pamphlets on the "Moral and Material Progress" of the state, wrote letters to the *Pioneer,* and created endowments in educational institutions. He visited England and delivered speeches on Hindu social reform before English ladies, "till all London cried: 'This is the most fascinating man we have ever met at dinner since cloths were first laid.'"[14] He also received many honorary degrees and he returned to India in a blaze of glory; the Viceroy paid a special visit to his state to confer upon him the coveted British title, K.C.I.E., and he became known as Sir Purun Dass, K.C.I.E. This was Purun Dass, the great man of action, the activist who brought glory to himself and his state through a ceaseless devotion to the cause of progress.

Then, the "miracle" suddenly took shape and Purun Dass "did a thing no Englishman would have dreamed of doing, for, so far as the world's affairs went, he died." It was an act of renunciation. He resigned his position of pomp and power, returned the medals, and took up the begging-bowl. As a holy man who has renounced all earthly pleasures he wore the ochre-colored dress of a Sannyasi in accordance with the religious Law. He had been "twenty years a youth, twenty years a fighter—though he had never carried a weapon in his life—and twenty years head of a household." Purun Dass was actually following the Hindu way of life, which is divided into four stages, and he arrived at the fourth and last stage of Sannyasa, the state of Renunciation.

Dewan Sir Purun Dass, K.C.I.E, left the capital city with an antelope skin and a bowl, since "India is the one place in the world where a man can do as he pleases and nobody asks why." Purun Dass became Purun Bhagat, the devotee of God and went his way to Kulu in search of divine truth and revelation. In Simla he saluted the Law of the traffic policeman because he had reverence for his own Higher Law. He followed the Himalaya-Tibet road and he "was alone with himself, walking, wondering, and thinking, his eyes on the ground, and his thoughts with the cloud." He saw a village in the valley and was impressed by the serene peace of the place. "Here shall I find peace," he exclaimed and bowed to the earth. He had at last come to the place destined for him—"the silence and the space. After this time stopped, and he, sitting at the mouth of the shrine, could not tell whether he were alive or dead." [15] In this serene shrine Purun Bhagat made friends with the animals and birds. The big monkeys of the Himalayas, the langurs; the big deer, bara-singha; the musk-deer; and the Himalayan black bear, Sona, all became Purun's companions. Purun's miracle was dra-matically displayed in his affectionate association with these animals and birds. Minaul, the pheasant, came to play with him. The villagers respected him and fed him.

On one dark, stormy, rainy night the animals came to warn Purun Bhagat of the impending danger of a landslide. He realized that "the langur's eyes were full of things that he could not tell," and, guessing the coming landslide, he bravely stepped out of the shrine into the wild night. He was now on a mission to save the villagers from death. He ran from house to house, waking people up and asking them to climb the highest ground to save themselves. He leaned against the barasingha and his powers of the old days were revived. He was no longer a holy man but became Sir Purun Dass, Prime Minister of a State, for a while. He knew how to command and organize people, and he performed his duties with great power and alacrity. At last the big deer, on whom Purun leaned, stopped in the pinewood, and the holy man whispered to the barasingha, "Stay with me, Brother. Stay— till—I—go!"

Purun Bhagat died. His life had found fulfillment in this last great mission. The langurs wailed, the Sona moaned, the barasingha kept vigil over Purun Bhagat "sitting cross-legged, his back against a tree, his crutch under his armpit, and his face turned to the north-east." The villagers, who were rescued from certain death, raised a memorial to Purun Bhagat, a shrine, without knowing that the holy man was once Sir Purun Dass, K.C.I.E, and a Prime Minister. His life completed a circle, it began in Kulu and ended there in the serene atmosphere of the divine Himalayas.

Purun Dass was an activist and Purun Bhagat a man of contemplation and devotion. In his character this growth shows a transformation from an activist into a man of god. He achieves a new dimension of the awareness of the divine through renunciation of the world and becomes a real savior of men. Within the structure of the story, the swift movement in the earlier part of the story is changed into a slow motion of divine intensity in the latter part of the story. Words seem to wade through the still waters of Purun Bhagat's existence.

The meaning of Purun Bhagat's miracle lies in realizing the significance of this transformation and relating it to the mode of Kipling's art. " 'The Miracle of Purun Bhagat' was beyond me," wrote J. M. S. Tompkins. "I did not understand what was happening." [16] What exactly is happening in "Purun Bhagat" is described by Kipling as a miracle, and the miracle is not so much that Purun Dass has become Purun Bhagat overnight but that he commenced his search with love for all men and animals. The great man of action has become a greater man of contemplation and aimed at synthesizing the concretions and abstractions of life. Purun Bhagat, writes K. R. Srinivasa Iyengar, "was a St. Francis re-enacting the drama of common friendliness and fellowship with man, beast and all nature." [17] In the character and personality of Purun Bhagat the Christian values are subtly synthesized with those of the Hindu way of life.

The miracle of Purun Bhagat is also, in part, the miracle of the growth of Kipling's art. Kipling too, like Purun, was a great lover of animals and visualized their communion with men. He believed, as the early Purun did, in the concretion of activism, from which his art sprang. Thus the concrete and the abstract, the real and the ideal, body and soul are harmonized in the unity of Kipling's vision.

In "Without Benefit of Clergy" the artist in Kipling emerges as a writer of dream and reality. This aspect of Kipling as an artist is woven into the fabric of the story which is marked by two worlds—the house of Ameera overlooking the city, with a courtyard full of marigolds, and Holden's bachelor bungalow with its "unlovely" life-style. In the lovely rooms of the first house Holden was king of all he surveyed, and

Ameera the queen. Holden was leading a "double life" as he passed from one world to the other. Ameera was wild with delight as she was expecting a baby, and even her money-minded mother was pleased at the prospect of this new arrival. Holden came to Ameera to break the unhappy news that the government "with singular care, had ordered him out of the station for a fortnight on special duty." There was a verbal version of the order emphasizing the fact that Holden should consider himself "lucky in being a bachelor and a free man." In this way the two worlds seem great opposites and Holden is really divided between them. One world may be generally described as romantic since it is based on Holden's deep love for Ameera, the Muslim girl, who is passionately devoted to him. Holden had in fact bought her from her avaricious mother, but his relationship with Ameera transcended the monetary level and culminated in true love. As against this romantic world, there is the every-day matter-of-fact world of British servicemen in India, marked by expediency, efficiency, and impersonal attachment to the idea of empire. John Holden is part of the activistic bureaucracy devoted to administration, and yet he is also romantic lover. The voice of his newborn babe "sent all his blood into the apple of his throat" and he reassured Ameera of his deep passion for her: "Yea. I love as I have loved, with all my soul. Lie still, pearl, and rest." The language of love of John and Ameera is marked by romantic passion and imagery and the idiom is derived from original Hindustani expressions often used by Indians in such contexts. John calls himself Ameera's "worshipper," [18] and Ameera declares that she is servant and slave and the dust under his feet. They name their son Tota (a parrot), who symbolizes the climax of their mutual happiness.

Kipling, it appears, is slowly building up the tragic passages in the narrative structure through scene and image. Holden fills out a telegram for Pir Khan, the gatekeeper, and then returns to his headquarters with "the sensations of a man who has attended his own funeral." After the birth of the child Holden acted out the ritual of killing the two goats, as sacrifice to safeguard the life of his son. But, in the process the raw blood spurted over his riding boots. The club secretary saw it and exclaimed, "Great goodness, man, it's blood!" On the auspicious Friday, Ameera settles herself in John's arms and the atmosphere is warm and stuffy. "The dry earth is lowing like a cow for the rain." She asks him to count the stars, but the sky is overcast. Then she tried to play the *sitar* and sing a song of Rajah Rasalu but instead sings a rhyme of the crow.

Kipling shows that the ecstasy of fulfillment, of the love of Ameera and Holden, was short-lived. Tota died and Ameera wept bemoaning her fate. On Tota's death Ameera "at the end of each weary day" led Holden "through the hell of self-questioning reproach," which is the fate of those who lose their children. Ameera, too, became a victim of cholera.

The image of the stars is central to the narrative content since Ameera, John, and their son are all involved in a compelling, ruthless, unkind circle of destiny. The tragic world in "Without Benefit of Clergy" is a lyrical presentation of man's unequal confrontation with an indifferent and unkind universe. As Elliot L. Gilbert has perceptively pointed out, the story "is not just a sentimental idyll," but its theme is "nothing less than the enormous hostility of the universe," which is "blundering, directionless and very nearly incapable of supporting human life." [19]

"Without Benefit of Clergy" is almost Shakespearean in its tone and temper, and the world of John and Ameera is a minor variation, in the context of nineteenth-century India, of the world of Romeo and Juliet. Love triumphs only after the body, the perishable clay, is consumed in the fires lit by fate. "Without Benefit of Clergy" is also an indirect reflection on the futility of ritual, and Ameera's love for Holden transcends all narrow ritualistic limitations and reaches the reality of the human spirit. The story also shows, indirectly, the process of the emergence of Kipling's art. The world of Ameera is a dreamworld of love and romance, whereas the world of Holden is a world of hard work and unlovely surroundings. These two worlds come together by sheer chance and are separated by the cruelty of Fate. The prosaic world of facts is transformed into a poetical world of love and

lyricism and this progression in "Without Benefit of Clergy"·
is also the progression of Kipling as an artist.

The Indian's innate love for, and involvement with, children
is portrayed with greater tenderness and pity in "The Story
of Muhammad Din" than in "Without Benefit of Clergy."
Kipling shows great economy in expression in portraying
Imam Din's love for Muhammad Din and the Anglo-Indian
master's attachment for the "tiny, plump figure in a ridicu-
lously inadequate shirt." Whereas Ameera's love for Tota,
her child, finds intense lyrical expression in language, Imam
Din's affection for his son is shown in phrases which are
terse and concentric. Even the exchanges between the Anglo-
Indian Sahib and the little boy are limited to briefest expressions, "*Talaam Tahib*," and "*Salaam, Muhammad Din.*"
Yet the tenderness and delicacy of human relationships is
beautifully portrayed in this very brief story. The boy was
punished by his father for having entered the Sahib's room.
The boy sobbed and said, "It is true my name is Muhammad
Did, *Tahib*, but I am not a *budmash*, I am a *man*!" The child
busied himself in the garden with broken pieces of bricks
and china. His act of half burying the Sahib's old polo-ball
in dust is a piece of dramatic irony as it is a premonition of
his own burial by his father. The accidental trampling by
the Sahib of the little boy's handiwork in the garden is also
an event which casts its shadows on Muhammad Din's small
world. He was always alone and always crooning to himself.
He was told the Sahib was not really angry and that he was
free to rebuild his palace. He designed it on a grand scale,
but suddenly the fever claimed him. And the last scene is an
accentuation of the tragic suffering of the father, Imam Din.
The Sahib "met on the road to the Mussulman burying-
ground Imam Din, accompanied by one other friend, carrying in his arms, wrapped in a white cloth, all that was left of
little Muhammed Din." [20]

This is one of the most terse descriptions of death in
Kipling's fiction in which is concentrated great and deep
passion for an offspring. The words, like those of Hamlet
spoken to the queen, become daggers and administer stabs

to human consciousness and create a powerful effect on human sensibility. The inscrutable ways of destiny are thus worked out into the small, sad and still world of Muhammad Did. Imam Din's love for Muhammad Din is very similar to Gino Carella's love for his son in E. M. Forster's *Where Angels Fear to Tread* (1905). Forster dramatically presents the scene in which Gino washes his baby. Miss Caroline Abbott who came to take away the baby, on seeing Gino so fond of the child, gave up her attempt.[21] Harriet, the baby's aunt, could not realize the truth of the baby and thought it was merely an object to be carried home like a bundle. The baby dies in an accident and the scene is as pathetic as the one in which Imam Din is carrying the dead body of his son, wrapped in white cloth, to the burial place.

The delicacy of emotional response between father and son, Imam Din and Muhammad Din, is also extended to the relationship between the Sahib and the boy, because it is through the Sahib's consciousness that we get a glimpse of the love between father and son. To interpret the Sahib's loving response to the Indian boy as an attitude of "condescension,"[22] as K. Bhaskar Rao has done, seems to me a case of oversimplification, since these relationships transcend the narrow racial or political barriers and become truly human. "The Story of Muhammad Din" is the finest example of Kipling's art in miniature. It is a delicate and sensitive painting of the dreamy, lovely boy confronted with his tragic destiny.

The synthesis of dream and reality is nowhere so pervasively reflected in Kipling's creative cosmos as in the beautifully designed story, "The Brushwood Boy." It depicts the pure dreams of George Cottar, of his childhood, adulthood, and of his stay in subaltern's quarters in India. As a three-year-old he saw a policeman on the Downs in a dream. He told stories to himself as a child and this became a new power within him. He dreamt of the prince and the princess who peopled his stories. When he was seven, he began to see ghosts which were thrilling. In his dreams skeletons danced bone by bone. At an entertainment he saw a girl sitting by him, and she seemed like the girl in *Alice in Wonderland*. When he came to Brushwood pines he saw her waiting for him, her hair combed off her forehead, like those of Alice. This is the sketch of the dreamworld of George as a child and an adolescent.

George Cotter leads a divided life and the other side of his personality is developed in the public school and later in his army career. He had his share of cricket and football in the Lower Third in the public school and this experience did not encourage dreaming. The next phase of his life unrolled itself in India, where he played polo and experienced "utter loneliness." [23] George began to dream again: dreams of innocence and experience filled his psyche. They always began in Brushwood pine and sometimes ended near Hongkong. He also did the day's work with great sincerity and alacrity and in his person the preoccupation with hard work was combined with the involvement with dreams. This was, in essence, his "double life," which was exposed to the charms of Mrs. Zuleika on the steamer bound for home.

The return to England was in a sense a return to the charm of Brushwod pines. His parents welcomed him heartily but his mother was puzzled by George's utter inexperience of women and his professed devotion to the prose of his profession "a man has all his work cut out for him to keep abreast of his profession, and my days are always too full to let me lark about half the night." George met Miriam, stared at her, "the Brushwood girl! I know her!" They went riding and George told Miriam: "I knew! You are you. Oh, I *knew* you'd come someday; but I didn't know you were you in the least till you spoke." [24] George dreamt of this girl in his childhood and met her now in his father's home. Thus the world of his dreams is brought into association with the world of his reality.

"The Brushwood Boy" is an extraordinary, almost unique, story of Kipling's, not merely because it portrays a series of George's dreams but also the growth of Kipling as an artist. Kipling's art grows out of the tension between two opposites —the world of facts and the world of spirit. These two opposites are also reflected in the divided self of George Cotter.

"The Gardener," the last story in *Debits and Credits*, written in 1925, is one of the most intricately designed and effectively rendered stories of Kipling. Its genesis could be traced to an intensely emotional phase of Kipling's life, the loss of his son, John, in the war and the painful uncertainty that surrounded his son's death. Kipling's visits to Ronen Cemetery provided the immediate setting and substance to the story which is marked by his overwhelming feeling of compassion.

That art lies in concealing art may be a half-truth but no story of Kipling demonstrates this view more powerfully than "The Gardener." It is a story of intense and moving passion, but the words hardly express it. The silences in "The Gardener" are more eloquent than speech and the gaps more expressive than complete sentences. Some of the details of Helen Turrell's life were public property, but not all. The village knew that Helen stood heroically by her brother's son and brought him to a happy home from France. But her actions in France are shrouded in mystery. We are told that she paid the passage of the child and the nurse from Bombay, nursed the baby through an attack of dysentery at Marseilles, dismissed the unsatisfactory nurse, and at last returned home "thin and worn but triumphant." [25] There is a tinge of irony to these adjectives as they probably suggest her state of pregnancy and the birth of an illegitimate son.

It is Helen Turrell's confrontation with her own self that is central to the theme of "The Gardener." She is consciously wearing a mask that she unconsciously is trying to remove. Michael had "the Turrell forehead, broad, low, and well shaped," and his mouth "was somewhat better cut than the family type," but Helen, "who would concede nothing good to his mother's side, vowed he was a Turrell all over." Helen's refusal to concede anything good to Michael's mother is a confrontation with her own self, strengthened by the feeling that there is no one "to contradict" her. The irony of the situation is sharply focused on the scene in which Michael wishes to call her Mummy and she explained that "she was only his auntie." She agreed to being called Mummy only at bedtime, which was a dent in the mask, but the dominant note is one of secrecy and suppression of self. Helen's contention that "it's always best to tell the truth" is ironical since she herself is consciously trying to suppress it. Michael's childlike anger expressed in "And when I'm dead I'll hurt you worse!" is a foreboding of the future and breaks through Helen's "stammered defences." Michael was to have gone up to Oxford, but he went to the war theater in France instead. A shell-splinter killed him on the spot and another shell destroyed a wall the ruins of which were all spread over his body making identification difficult. The thread of this loss of physical identity is woven into the fabric of the story. Michael was reported missing, and a long correspondence resulted in utter frustration. Later the news of the death came and Helen's "world had stood still." His body was re-interred in Hagenzeele Third Military Cemetery and Helen decided to visit the grave. Helen's meeting with Mrs. Scarsworth is significant because she realized the other lady's identical problem of breaking the fences of falsehood: "Because I'm so tired of lying." But Helen could not confess because she could not really rid herself of her mask.

The last scene in "The Gardener" is indeed very touching, partly because of its subdued tone. Helen Turrell is a twentieth-century Mary Magdalene in search of the stone of the sepulcher, and the lost identity of her son. This scene is obviously related to the story of Magdalene in the Gospel of St. John (20:15). Jesus appeared before her and said, " 'Woman, why weepest thou?' . . . She, supposing him to be the gardener, saith unto him, 'Sir, if thou have borne him hence, tell me where thou hast laid him, and I will take him away.' " The biblical parallel is obvious, and clearly implied in the title, but Helen Turrell's predicament is different from the problem of Magdalene and is expressed in her question to the gardener at the cemetery. Helen saw that a man "knelt behind a line of headstones—evidently a gardener, for he was firming a young plant in the soft earth." He asked her, "Who are you looking for?"

"Lieutenant Michael Turrell—my nephew," said Helen slowly and word for word, as she had many thousands of times in her life.

The man lifted his eyes and looked at her with infinite compassion before he turned from the fresh-sown grass toward the naked black crosses.

"Come with me," he said, "and I will show you where your son lies."

When Helen left the cemetery she turned for a last look. In the distance she saw the man bending over his young plants, and she went away, supposing him to be the gardener.[26]

The gardener by substituting the word "son" for "nephew" at last confirmed the pent-up truth in Helen's heart. It was the first voice of the world without, that Helen heard, which echoed the world within.

Rudyard Kipling's involvement with the daemon becomes the origin of many of his supernatural stories. "The Phantom 'Rickshaw" was the first of such stories in which Kipling came very close to his daemon, which became a perennial source of his creativity. Alluding to the personal daemon of Aristotle and other great writers Kipling said that "this is the doom of the Makers—their Daemon lives in their pen" [27] and that "If he be absent or sleeping, they are even as other men." The daemon certainly lives in Kipling's pen and it came out openly first in "The Phantom 'Rickshaw." Referring to this story, Kipling writes that "some of it was weak, much was bad and out of key; but it was my first serious attempt to think in another man's skin." It is interesting to note that this association between Kipling and the daemon also becomes one of the processes of his Becoming, since he tries to enter into another man's skin. He allowed his pen to take charge and the stories took shape. His daemon was with him in the *Jungle Books* and *Puck of Pook's Hill*, and he tried to harmonize his inspirations with the promptings of the daemon.

Kipling's close association with the Masonic Lodge [28] indirectly kindled his interest in the spiritual and the esoteric. Moreover, he was deeply involved in the supernatural atmosphere generated by the Indian tradition of fairy tales. As a child with a precocious imagination, he heard such stories from Meeta, the Indian servant in Bombay. His family tradition and religious beliefs also strengthened his imaginative inclination toward the superantural. "To one in whom the Wesleyan and Pre-Raphaelite traditions met," writes Thomas R. Henn, "the other world, and its potential power and mystery, combined to produce the shudders of awe." [29] This interest in the spirit world molded Kipling's literary taste for the exploration of the supernatural. His perennial interest in the working of the human psyche and man's abnormalities also acted as a stimulant to the writing of ghost stories.

Although the structure of "The Phantom 'Rickshaw" is weak—it is not a tightly organized tale—its various episodes are woven around a frame which is the favorite Kipling device in his art of the short story. At first the substance of his stories seems to be sprawling, yet it is linked with the basic framework. It appears that Kipling has certainly conceived the frame before he begins to write the first word of the story. The frame in "The Phantom 'Rickshaw" is molded by the central concept of exploring the consciousness of Jack Pansay and depicting the daemon that has taken hold of his person. This device implies that the story, and the main events and characters in it have to be portrayed from Jack's point of view. Jack Pansay is at the center and his psyche which reflects his relationship with Mrs. Keith-Wessington and later with Kitty Mannering is the principal object of Kipling's exploration. Jack Pansay on his return voyage to Bombay from England has fallen in love with a Mrs. Keith-Wessington. It was "an ill-omened attachment" and soon the "fire of straw burnt itself out to a pitiful end." Though she continued to feel a strong passion for Jack, he was sick of her presence, disgusted, and totally disillusioned. He hated her, yet she continued to appeal to him in the hope of reconciliation. Jack soon fell in love with Kitty Mannering and they were engaged. Mrs. Wessington was told of this development and within a week she died of grief. Jack and Kitty were now madly in love and he wished to buy her an engagement ring. They went to Hamilton's in Simla on April 15, 1885 and he bought a lovely ring. On the way back Jack's eye was caught by the sight of "four *hampanies* in 'magpie' livery, pulling a yellow paneled . . . 'rickshaw." He cried that they were Mrs. Wessington's *hampanies*, but Kitty was unable to see them. " 'What? Where?' she asked. 'I can't see them anywhere.' " Jack saw Mrs. Wessington, "handerchief in hand, and golden head bowed on her breast" in the 'rickshaw. The phantom 'rickshaw appeared many times and Jack consulted Dr. Heatherlegh, who treated him for eyes, brain, and liver. The phantom had taken possession of him, and in spite of his attempts to regain normalcy, he continued to be haunted by it and the lady. The episode ends in frustration and breakup of the engagement with Kitty Mannering. Jack tries to look into his psyche and confesses pathetically "Yet as surely as ever a man was done to death by the Powers of Darkness, I am that man." [30]

Kipling's mode of exposition employs a narrator who, in fact, lays down the design of the story. The narrator tells us that Jack Pansay was in a state of "high fever" while he wrote this story and that the "blood-and-thunder Magazine diction he adopted did not calm him." The narrator received the manuscript before Jack died and the real story began at this stage. The mode of Kipling's narration is indeed loose and weak and the characters and events seem to fly past the protagonist, Jack Pansay. "The Phantom 'Rickshaw" is one of Kipling's very early stories and therefore the want of a tighter organization and a firmer grip can be attributed to the early, immature phase of his growth as an artist. He also uses clichés in this story, such as "There are more things in heaven and earth," "dark labyrinths of doubt," which further weaken its impact.

"The Strange Ride of Morrowbie Jukes" is a remarkable advance on "The Phantom 'Rickshaw" in terms of theme, atmosphere, and intent. Jukes, by sheer accident, stumbled upon a village "where the Dead who did not die but might not live," have erected their town. Jukes, who is a Civil Engineer, involuntarily visited this village, and a treacherous sand slope prevented his escape. He meets Gunga Dass, the telegraph-master, as a "withered skeleton, turbanless and almost naked," who teaches him how to catch crows. There is a gruesome description of this despicable village of the dead. Jukes is at last rescued by his faithful servant Dunnoo, who followed the pony-track and hauled his master out of the hideous land.

Its theme is Man's confrontation with the inescapable pit, and its atmosphere is really gruesome. The inhabitants are those who were thought to be dead but who revived on their way to the burning-ghâts, and their experiences only heighten the effect of the hideous atmosphere. Man's predicament in relation to the pit of human horror, the hell within, which is a characteristic of Kipling's later phase, is foreshadowed in "The Strange Ride of Morrowbie Jukes."

"My Own True Ghost Story" is one of Kipling's rare attempts to rationalize Western man's experience of ghosts in the East. The sequence of the supernatural is built up only to find its climax in the revelation of the natural. "This story," writes Kipling, "deals entirely with ghosts." The narrator of the story was camping at a Katmal dâk-bungalow in India where "a fair proportion of the tragedy" of Anglo-Indian life unrolls itself. The old *khansamah* went to bring food for the Sahib; meanwhile the narrator explored the bungalow which had three rooms besides his own. After his meal the narrator went to bed but soon saw shadows in the room. Then he heard the sound of the doors in the next room. He listened, and a billiard game seemed to be in progress. The pity was that the next room was too small to hold a billiard table, yet he clearly heard the whirring sound of the billiard ball. Next morning the old *khansamah* told him that the house was a game room for billiards during the days of the railway's construction and that the engineers played there. One fat engineer, who was addicted to whisky, suddenly died while playing billiards on that spot. It had been one big hall then, which was later partitioned into three rooms. Thus, at last, the narrator had had the satisfaction of meeting with a ghost. But he stayed on for the night "while the wind and the rat and the sash and the window-bolt played a ding-dong," and then suddenly the wind died, the billiards stopped, and the narrator ruined his "one genuine, hall-marked ghost story."

This perfectly natural explanation of the phenomena of ghosts brings out ironically the significance of the adjective "true" in the title "My Own True Ghost Story."

Kipling's stories about ghosts or supernatural beings form part of a pattern governed by his attitude to life. All his life as a creative artist Kipling was involved in the sense of the enigmatic and the mysterious which assumed various shapes and forms. His speculative tendency was concerned as much with the life of the body as with the life of the spirit. He made various attempts to trace the goings-on between the world of men and that of spirits. This interlinking gives various dimensions to his ghost stories.

"The Lost Legion" is a story of the tribal region of the North-West Frontier Province in India where the Goorkhas and the British soldiers are engaged in a campaign to subdue the rebels. The English would block the hillside of the valley and the Goorkhas the gorge, thus creating a death trap for Mullah's men. Lieutenant Halley heard mysterious voices and the cavalry was dumbfounded. Amidst thunder and rain a voice came from the watchtower, "Oh, Hafiz Ullah!" The echoes repeated "ha-la-la" and, then, the answer followed: "What is it, Shahbaz Khan?" and Halley began to shiver under his rock and saw an Afghan soldier tumbling into his arms. The Afghan was shocked, " 'The Rissala! The dead Rissala!' he gasped. 'It is down there!' " This Afghan was terrified of "the Ghost Regiment," which was lost during the rebellion of 1857. The regiment of Native Irregular Horse, stationed in Peshawar, was almost liquidated by the local Afghan tribesmen who wished to take away their uniforms and equipment. This carnage of the "Ghost Regiment" that took place thirty years earlier is now relived and reexperienced by the Goorkhas and the British soldiers. Thus the "Lost Legion" is re-created as a disturbing psychological phenomenon and part of the supernatural world.

The technique of these ghost or horror stories is more that of a string of anecdotes than that of a well-conceived tale. Stories such as "For One Night Only," "Thurinda," "Of Those Called," and "Sleipner" are mostly anecdotes built around a bizarre theme, whereas longer narratives such as "Return of Imray" and "By Word of Mouth" have a larger canvas which is conditioned by realistic setting. The mode of narration is marked by an informal and casual touch and the structure is not tightly organized. The ultimate impression created by these stories is one of horror.

"In the House of Suddhoo" the horror of black magic becomes the central theme and the characters, Suddhoo, Janoo, Azizun, and the seal-cutter revolve round it. Suddhoo's son at Peshawar was ill, and the seal-cutter arranged to receive news of his state of health by telegram. He then made capital out of it by reporting, for a price, on the son's condition each day. Kipling portrays the gruesome sight of the black *jadoo* as manipulated by the seal-cutter. The narrator "looked at the basin, and saw bobbing in the water, the dried, shriveled, black head of a native baby—open eyes, open mouth, and shaved scalp." The view that the Government "rather patronizes the Black Art" has a ring of irony to it.

"A Wayside Comedy" is a story with a highly complicated pattern which suggests parallelism with the Bible and more significantly with modern existential literature. Kashima, the station in the hills, is described as "the Garden of Eden." There was a misunderstanding between Mr. and Mrs. Boulte which threatened to disrupt their home. "When Samson broke the pillars of Gaza, he did a little thing, and one not to be compared with the deliberate pulling down of a woman's homestead about her own ears." [31] These references strengthen the view that Kipling in "A Wayside Comedy" was re-creating a parable, in narrative form, of the Fall and Redemption, as already suggested by Louis L. Cornell.[32] To me, the significance of "A Wayside Comedy" does not very much lie in this scriptural context but rather in the spirit of modern twentieth-century man which underlies its theme and structure. Bonamy Dobrée has rightly emphasized the idea of loneliness [33] which is the main feature of the world depicted in the story. Elsie B. Adams, in a discerning essay,[34] has pointed out the similarities between Kipling's "A Wayside

Comedy" and Jean-Paul Sartre's play *Huis-clos* (*No Exit*, 1944). "A Wayside Comedy" is indeed informed of the tragic spirit that emanates from the isolation, loneliness, and frustration of man. Even the very first sentence of the story unfolds this basic issue: "Fate and the Government of India have turned the Station of Kashima into a prison; and, because there is no help for the poor souls who are now lying there in torment, I write this story." The description of Kashima as a prison is symptomatic of a segment of modern civilization. The use of the words *fate, prison, poor souls,* and *torment* suggests a movement of feeling and a movement of thought which grow into the structure of the story. The isolation of Kashima is almost complete; it "never goes to Nar-karra"; it stays within its own circle of the hills.

The torment in Kashima is caused by the arrival of Mrs. Vansuythen who spurns Mr. Boulte's love. Mr. and Mrs. Boulte overheard Mrs. Vansuythen saying that Kurrel didn't care a whit for Mrs. Boulte and she fainted. The narrative is further complicated by the curiosity of the characters to know who exactly are the legitimate lovers of Mrs. Vansuythen and Mrs. Boulte. Both Boulte and Captain Kurrel are confronted with the predicaments of their own making and all the characters in the story suffer except the genial Major Van-suythen who is unaware of the emotional undercurrents.

"A Wayside Comedy" portrays the ruinous aspect of love. The spirit of Restoration comedy seems to hang over Ka-shima, though it is only a small hill-station in India. Kipling universalizes the theme and it no longer remains a play of desire and disgust of the characters in Kashima only, but an exposition of these basic emotions of man in all places, for all time.

"Mrs. Bathurst" is indeed one of the most obscure stories of Kipling, but its obscurities and complexities have been ex-amined and analyzed by critics at such great length that any further elaboration runs the risk of being repetitive. The two aspects of its art, the form and technique of "Mrs. Bathurst," have evoked a great deal of critical explication. C. A. Bodel-sen has analyzed [35] the cinematographic technique in "Mrs.

Bathurst" making it a "fundamental clue" to its meaning.
Elliot L. Gilbert has perceptively analyzed the philosophical
theme of the story, "the fortuitousness of life," in relation to
Vickery's experience, and traced the connection between "the
untidiness of the universe" and the "function" of Kipling's
style and its obscurities.

The desertion of Vickery is central to the narrative structure of "Mrs. Bathurst" and it is the subject of discussion between Pyecroft and Inspector Hooper. Vickery was considered
a balanced man until he fell in love with Mrs. Bathurst, a
hotelkeeper from New Zealand. He could not resist the charm
of Mrs. Bathurst, who was a widow, and she on her part was
also deeply involved. Their relationship must have been
passionate, yet this is an aspect of the human predicament
which is part of the obscurity of the story. The four men in
the railroad car are attempting to reconstruct the events of
the last phase of Vickery's life and their versions also contribute to the complexity of the story.

The manner of Vickery's death is much too improbable,
and the identity of the second tramp—whether it was Mrs.
Bathurst herself—is shrouded in mystery. She is, as J. M. S.
Tompkins has suggested, a vehicle of blind power. She
represents the element of chance which results in the death
of Vickery, and the irony of the situation is that she is
totally unaware of it. Mrs. Bathurst thus unconsciously becomes the instrument of the blind fury of fate.

Mrs. Bathurst was dead when Pyecroft had watched her
in the film. Pyecroft's moral lapse is revealed in his unwilling-
ness to marry her because he does not want to desert his
pregnant wife. And the real victim of love is Mrs. Bathurst, as
pointed out by Bodelsen, and not Vickery. Equating the
second tramp with Mrs. Bathurst is, according to P. W.
Brock, a critical fallacy. He believes that Kipling deliberately
omitted certain facts because "the omitted would strengthen
the story and make people feel more than they understood." [36]
In this context the problem of clearing the mystery of the
second body is superfluous, nor is it really necessary to specify
the whereabouts of Mrs. Bathurst. A great deal of criticism
on this count suggesting that the second body was that of

Mrs. Bathurst is purely speculative and contributes to the obscurity of the meaning and complexity of the plot of "Mrs. Bathurst." However, the story is great because it makes a powerful impact on the reader and its obscurities and complexities contribute to the richness of its structure and design.

In conclusion, the question should be raised briefly about Kipling's rank as a short-story writer. A short story must create a single effect upon the sensibility of the reader, of the intensity of an incident or a character. The stages in its structure include the rising action culminating in a climax or crisis followed by a denouement. The theme of the short story implies its total meaning. Character delineation and creation of atmosphere are the other important elements of its structure. These are some of the essentials of the short story as a form.

Does Kipling achieve this objective of creating one, single, unified impression? The answer is that Kipling does not always achieve this objective, yet he is a great craftsman. This primary objective of the art of the short story is sometimes vitiated in his work by Kipling's habit of allowing surplusage in the content of his stories. Yet, he succeeds as a great writer because his stories present his conception of life and also because they offer such excellent character-delineation and achieve verisimilitude. As a craftsman Kipling is great, but as an artist he is even greater.

6

Poetry

Recognition of the integral nature of Kipling's creative genius is an indispensable preliminary for the revaluation of his poetry. His was a unified sensibility and a single, indivisible talent. His achievement in different fields of writing cannot, therefore, be compartmentalized with rigidly disparate canons of critical assessment. His peculiar qualities and failings as a writer are not confined to a particular genre. They are sufficiently uniform to suggest a pervasive pattern to evaluate his stature as a creative artist. From this perspective, the common—if uncritical—assumption that Kipling was a gifted storyteller but a third-rate poet is a consequence of the failure to recognize the basic unity behind his achievement. The poetical qualities of Kipling cannot be dissociated from his characteristics as a skillful writer of prose fiction.

These divergent criteria for assessment stem, in fact, from the unequal nature of Kipling's achievement. Like Wordsworth, Kipling was an unequal writer and distinctly gains by judicious selection. This accounts for the several anthologies of his prose and verse. But this uneven achievement was the consequence of a number of obvious reasons. Kipling began his career as a journalist and his writings—particularly his early creative writing—carry the imprint of journalistic casualness and tour de force. Moreover, he was a prolific writer and his writing was consequently diffuse in nature. Finally, the most crucial factor was his moodiness. He was a man of unpredictable temperament and this unmistakably affected his writing.

This uneven nature of Kipling's achievement is particularly pronounced in his poetry. This led to diverse and often contradictory evaluations. He has been derided as a poet of jingles and dismissed as a composer of commonplace ballads and hymns. He is, it is still further held, all jingoistic sound and imperialistic fury signifying nothing but the verbosity of hollow Victorian and Edwardian milieu. As against this denunciation, Kipling is described both as a romantic and as a poet, in Bonamy Dobrée's phrase, "of actuality." [1]

These conflicting assessments, however, do not detract from the fact that Kipling was an immensely popular poet who cannot be nonchalantly consigned to the limbo of oblivion. Kipling's popularity can be adduced by any number of instances. Roger Burlingame recalls a touching incident in his life during the First World War in France. He, along with other American soldiers, was preparing to leave for home but was suddenly attacked by the mortal flu. He met a quartermaster captain, who seemed a typical barrack-room creation, and who was having a similar attack. They decided to have a bottle of cognac. This captain had the appearance of one who had never read a book in his life. After a while he said he would like to sing and he sang "Danny Deever" through. And then he recited "Mandalay," "Fuzzy-Wuzzy," and "Gunga Din," completely and without mistake. He also remembered Kipling's stories by heart. "Perhaps it was the cognac that warded off the flu," writes Roger Burlingame. "I like to think it was the presence of Kipling cheering us on that wet dawn." [2] This incident indicates the extraordinary impact of Kipling on the Edwardian sensibility.

Yet Kipling's very popularity has, strangely enough, interposed a peculiar barrier to a genuine assessment of his poetry since popularity is often bracketed with mediocrity. Moreover, unlike modern poets, he was never a poet of a particular coterie, a select group of highbrow intellectuals. His conception of poetry was traditional in the sense that he believed it to be an instrument of direct participation between the reader and the poet. Poetry for him was not merely a means for self-expression but a means of communication in which the reader has a definite role assigned to him. In this regard, a modern poet is inclined to say, "If you do not understand me, so much the worse for you," whereas Kipling would assert, "If you do not understand me, so much the worse for *me*." Complete rapport between the poet and the reader thus becomes, an important element in Kipling's poetry, particularly in regard to his choice of poetic forms. A poet who aims at direct communication is likely to find only certain verse forms—such as the ballad—suitable for his poetic needs.

Kipling's poetry is highly eloquent, almost oracular. Therefore, not only contemporary preference, but his own poetic intention, made him choose the form of the ballad. The word *ballad* is derived from the Italian *ballare* (meaning "to dance"). Generally, it is a traditional story told lyrically. It has a variety of tonal implications: moral, spiritual, and political. The ballad measure is the quartrain stanza or the old fourteener divided into two parts. The second and the fourth lines rhyme and sometimes the first and the third lines as well. Kipling's ballads, however, are in tune with the restricted form of the ballad as the narrative lyric, subtantially molded by the norms of the nineteenth-century poetry. Morevoer, he shows himself a master craftsman in such ballads as "The Explorer" and "The Ballad of East and West." As Lionel Stevenson has pointed out, "Kipling has written the only sestina in English that has poetic merit." [3] In handling this fixed poetic form of six stanzas, of six lines each, and an *envoi* of three lines, Kipling shows consummate skill and precision.

The most predominant quality of Kipling's ballads is their musicality. He is a poet of apt sound which is truly rhythmic in the context in which it is employed. He is not an echo-poet borrowing from music halls or operas the rhythms or tunes of his poems. His poems follow the traditional folk-ballad rhythms and the words and music are truly integrated in them. There is no dichotomy between his words and their musicality and therefore his music, unlike Swinburne's, is not false. T. S. Eliot has perceptively commented [4] upon the false musicality of Swinburne's language in poetry, suggesting that his poetry has almost a drugging effect on his readers. Initially the reader is carried away by Swinburne's musical words, but after a time he returns to those words to know what they mean. But curiously he finds that Swinburne's musical words are divorced from meaning, and that they are even alienated from music itself. Swinburne thus creates, says T. S. Eliot, a hypnotic effect with his music. While the musicality in Swinburne has this fake exterior, in Kipling words and music are one thereby creating an enduring effect of rhythm.

Kipling's most important ballad, thematically, is the "The Ballad of East and West." This has often been misinterpreted as a poem articulating Kipling's basic attitude to contemporary racial and political problems. The very first lines of the ballad ("Oh East is East, and West is West, and never the twain shall meet") have acquired notoriety as affirming the essential incompatibility between East and West. This of course ignores the fact that Kipling himself, in the succeeding lines, contradicts this by stating unequivocally:

But there is neither East nor West, Border,
nor Breed, nor Birth,
When two strong men stand face to face, tho' they come
from the ends of the earth! [5]

Even an outline of the story is enough to underline the fact that Kipling, instead of voicing this alleged incompatibility, was in fact expressing his faith in the capacity of the two strong men to transcend these apparently irreconcilable categories. Kamal, the border Afghan, lifts the Colonel's horse. The Colonel's son goes to recover his father's horse. Kamal is impressed by the young man's bravery and returns the horse. The English boy gives the Afghan his pistol and the Afghan chief sends his son to serve in the Guides after taking "the oath of the Brother-in-Blood." Kipling obviously praises vitality, strength, physical and moral courage, and unflinching loyalty between two committed individuals. The thematic strand of the ballad thus is fairly complex.

The complexity of the poem also stems from the subtle changes which Kipling introduced into the actual events which form the basis of the ballad. The English Colonel in the poem, as pointed out by Karl W. Deutsch and Norbert

Wiener,[6] is Sir Robert Warburton, who is known as the founder of the Khyber Rifles. As historians of the Border Wars have noted,[7] Colonel Warburton was taken prisoner in Kabul in 1842 and he escaped through the regal intervention of an Afghan princess whom he later married. The hero of Kipling's poem is, in reality, Sir Warburton's son, Warburton, Jr., who was obviously half Afghan, half English. Quite ironically East and West had already met in the person of Warburton, Jr. and as such one of the two principal characters in the ballad nullifies the argument of the incompatibility of East and West. The major question is why Kipling chose to suppress the facts which were so out-of-step and exotic and why he remained content with showing the Colonel's son in the ballad as a pure Anglo-Saxon in Indian setting. The reasons, as suggested by Deutsch and Wiener, are much deeper than are readily apparent. Kipling faithfully followed the principal image of the literature of Imperialism in depicting closely contrasted relationships, white and black, superior and inferior, advanced and backward. This in-group feeling is central to the cerative expression of imperialism and it could be effectively shown only if one hero remains purely English and the other purely Afghan. Thus Kipling endeavored to synthesize this in-group feeling with the notion of the union of two powerful men who would overcome the barriers of East and West. This seems to be the process of resolving the main tension in the narrative on the acceptable criterion of strength and vitality.

The imperialistic theme of the "The Ballad of East and West" forms only a part of Kipling's creative response to the contemporary social and intellectual milieu. Another significant strand of his poetry springs from the romantic heritage of Victorian poetry. It is not romantic, however, in the sense in which Shelley's or Keats's poetry is considered romantic as an extraordinary development of imaginative sensibility or an expression of strange beauty and subtle sense of mystery. It is romantic in the sense in which Browning's poetry is. It is marked by an intellectual curiosity, by a conversational, informal tone and rhythm, and the drama of the experience of everyday life. The romantic Kipling is, thus, more in tune with the lingering romanticism of late Victorian and early Edwardian poets rather than with the early exuberance of the first or second generation of British romantic poets—Coleridge, Wordsworth, Shelley, Keats, and Byron. Moreover, Kipling's family association with the Pre-Raphaelites sustained his romantic temper, though he is quite outside, and even in the opposite ranks of, their circle. In my view Kipling's relationship with the romantic stream in English poetry has to be traced to the declining fortunes of romanticism in Victorian poetry. After the death of Byron and Coleridge romanticism was no longer a living force or a creative spark in English literature. Its energies were sapped by the growth of rationalism, commercialism, and the scientific movement of the Victorian age. The Victorian poets, Tennyson and Browning, endeavored to check the excesses of romanticism by subjecting it to the rigors of a classical discipline. Kipling arrived on the scene of English poetry at a time when the two major English poets were engaged in their task of discovering a balance between exuberant romanticism and the claims of classicism. Unlike Swinburne, Kipling does not join the procession of the "grave-diggers of romanticism." [8] He is very much apart and very individualistic in the response to the romantic traditions. This heterogeneous group of tendencies in late-Victorian poetry perhaps accounts for the fact that Kipling wrote some very romantic poems and also that, paradoxically, he is a realistically-inclined versifier.

These divergent modes of romanticism and realism are clearly discernible even in the first book of Kipling's poems, entitled *Departmental Ditties*. They are partly romantic in tone but they are also marked by the satirical tendencies of the early Kipling, subjected to divided and conflicting values. But they are uniformly distingiushed by an acute observation, a clarity, an effective scenic presentation, and a sharp, racy style which are in refreshing contrast to romantic gush and Victorian verbosity. Laughter, joviality, wit, and word-play, thus become the primary characteristics of Kipling in his early phase. "The Betrothed," for instance, is composed on the funny idea of the choice between a woman and a cigar. "You must choose between me and your cigar":

We quarreled about Havanas—we fought o'er a good cheroot,
And I know she is exacting, and she says I am a brute.[9]

Kipling's word-play in this verse is shown in his description of the poet's relationship with Maggie: "And the light of Days that have Been the dark of the Days that Are,/And Love's torch stinking and stale, like the butt of a dead cigar." He describes the gloom of his bachelor days being "flecked with the cheery light" and stumps that he "burned to Friendship and Pleasure and Work and Fight." Kipling is sometimes tempted by the weight and ponderousness of personification and his imagination harks back to eighteeenth-century neo-classical modes of personifying abstractions and satirizing human foibles.

In "The Plea of the Simla Dancers" the dancers of the hill station are shown as evoking the memories of "tuneful nights," "the witchery of flying feet," "wailing waltz," and "sparkling eyes," [10] all qualities of light verse in which Kipling excels as a craftsman. The early Kipling is a lover of valleys and dales, lakes and rivulets, and catches the wild beauty of the Indian landscape in Simla and elsewhere. In "An Old Song," the reference to "Tara Devi" watching the "lights o' Simla town" and to Kalka hills as "The everlasting Hills" [11] affords evidence of his love of nature. His descriptions of the moon in "The Moon of Other Days," besides showing his love of nature, seems to be an attempt to combine the East and the West in the poet's sensibility in phrases such as "Sainted Diana!" [12] The moon rises through the haze "Blood-red behind the sere *ferash*," [13] which is another attempt in the same direction. In translating "Certain Maxims of Hafiz," [14] the Persian poet, Kipling endeavors to render the effect of Eastern imagery and thought through the English language:

The temper of chums, the love of your wife, and a new
*   piano's tune—*
Which of the three will you trust at the end of an Indian
*   June?* [15]

The vagaries of men and women and the transitoriness of life are conveyed through typically Persian imagery in these renderings.

In spite of this love of nature and an exuberantly jovial attitude toward life, Kipling also wrote some poems which are marred by pseudo romanticism. For instance, his poem "To the Unknown Goddess" carries the stamp of the Pre-Raphaelite involvement with the physical, but it does not transcend a certain amount of wistful, though slightly false, longing:

Will you conquer my heart with your beauty; my soul going
out from afar?
Shall I fall to your hand as a victim of crafty and cautious
shikar? [16]

The pseudoromantic trend in Kipling is revealed when he describes the speaker in the poem "as a deer to the hand of the hunter" and envisages his beloved as a goddess, "Ah, Goddess! child, spinster, or widow," and calls himself "a young Pagan." He has addressed a poem to a goddess whom he has not yet seen. Similarly, the rivalry between a woman and a girl, on physical as well as psychological levels, is portrayed rather prosaically in "My Rival." A girl of seventeen with a "girlish blush" is jealous of the "constant cheek" of a mature woman of forty-nine.

> *The incense that is mine by right*
> *They burn befor Her shrine;*
> *And that's because I'm seventeen*
> *And She is forty-nine.*[17]

The image of the lover burning incense before his beloved's shrine is typically romantic though it also shows how Kipling tried to assimilate alien imagery into the traditional imagistic patterns of English poetry. Similarly, Kipling's description of Indian landscape catches the color and the rhythm of its peculiar elements. The haunting beauty of the hills at Simla, in India, is beautifully distilled in a single image in "The Lover's Litany":

> *Eyes of blue—the Simla Hills*
> *Silvered with the moonlight hoar;*
> *Pleading of the Waltz that thrills,*
> *Dies and echoes round Benmore.*[18]

The lover speaks of himself as "four times Cupid's debtor I—" who later becomes "bankrupt in quadruplicate." In "As the Bell Clinks" Kipling's "misty meditation" settles on the "vision of a comely maid" whom he had "worshipped dumbly" and adored "blindly" with adolescent passion. He says that "if a kiss had been imprinted" on this sweet maiden's cheek, it would "ha' saved a world of trouble!"[19] The pseudo-romantic trends of the youthful, adolescent Kipling are reflected in these light, airy, and witty poems of his early phase.

These themes of imperialism and romanticism apart, the artistic vision of Kipling as a poet is essentially that of an activist. His poetry is a vigorous expression of his positive philosophy of life. He is a poet of action and not of contemplation and in his imagination every thought, every dream, becomes a springboard for action. His heroes in poetry, therefore, are those who actively participate in the process of bettering this world. It is this pragmatic attitude which seems to me a fascinating quality of his vision as a poet. His world, like that of Browning, "is wondrous large" and it accommodates sinners as well as saints, princes as well as paupers, whites as well as blacks. In this regard Kipling has a striking similarity to Browning who had a definite influence on him. Kipling was fascinated by this sprawling humanity, the brave and boisterous world that he watched in his travels. This kindled his curiosity and provoked his intelligence, thereby powerfully influencing his vision as an artist:

> *Gawd bless this world! Whate'er she 'ath done—*
> *Excep' when awful long—I've found it good*
> *So write before I die, 'E liked it all!*[20]

These lines have striking similarity to Browning's *Fra Lippo Lippi* for whom the world is meat and drink, and is intensely good and boisterously alive:

This world's no blot for us,
Nor blank—it means intensely and means good:
To find its meaning is my meat and drink.[21]

This firm belief in activism is poetically expressed in "Galley Slave," "If," and several other poems eulogizing devotion to work, duty, and moral ideals. Man must dream, says
Kipling, but should not make dreams his master. He must
think, but not make thoughts his sole aim. If he can "fill the
unforgiving minute with sixty seconds' worth of distance
run," then he will be the master of all he surveys on the
earth and, what is more important, he will be a man. Even
in the satirical poem "Pagett, M.P." by ridiculing him
(Pagett) as a fluent liar who speaks of India's heat as the
"Asian Solar Myth," [22] Kipling is indirectly emphasizing the
British serviceman's sense of duty. Pagett called the poet a
"bloated Brahmin" and the poet in return called him one of
those "traveled idiots who duly misgovern the land." In "The
Sons of Martha" another aspect of activism, in relation to the
Machine, has been praised for its contribution to the building up of civilization and ensuring man's progress through
the ages.

Kipling's positive approach to the contemporary develop-
ments in science and technology is merely an extension of
his positivistic belief in progress. This is particularly evident
in "The Sons of Martha" (1907), which is a poetical expression of activism. He pays eloquent tribute to the pioneering work of engineers and technicians who say to the moun-
tains:

"Be ye remov'ed." They say to the lesser floods, "Be dry."
Under their rods the rocks reprov-ed—they are not
*   afraid of that which is high.*[23]

Their energy and their skill in engineering are employed for
the happiness of man and progress of civilization. They have
built roads and paths, on which are spilled their blood, the
sacrifice of workmen in the course of construction. What
sort of a road have these sons of Martha built?

> *Not as a ladder from earth to Heaven, not as a*
> *witness to any creed,*
> *But simple service simply given to his own kind*
> *in their common creed.*

These engineers do not preach that God's pity permits them "to drop their job when they dam'-well choose." The underlying irony of "The Sons of Martha" is shown in their sense of responsibility which goes unrecognized by the world. While it is their case "in all the ages to take the buffet and cushion the shock," the sons of Mary smile and are blessed. The biblical allusion to Martha, sister of Lazarus and Mary, who was rebuked by Jesus for doing housework while he talked with Mary (Luke 10:40), is beautifully woven into the fabric of the poem. The sons of Martha carry forward the tradition of the principle of housework, drab but essential, for the maintenance and upliftment of humanity. Unrecognized they toil for the happiness of men. These engineers, asserts Kipling, are activists engaged in the art of enriching civilization.

But Kipling, while recognizing the significance and utility of machines, is also aware of their limitations in relation to the divine law and the larger moral issues confronting man. In a poem entitled "The Secret of the Machines," the machines manufactured by men speak of their power over the elements of nature. These machines are the products of mechanical laws and therefore "are not built to comprehend a lie."

> *We are greater than the Peoples or the Kings—*
> *Be humble, as you crawl beneath our rods!—*
> *Our touch can alter all created things,*
> *We are everything on earth—except The Gods!* [24]

Similarly, in the "Dedication from *Barrack-Room Ballads*," Kipling offers a very eloquent tribute to the activists of his generation who sacrificed their all for the progress of this world. They are performing a divine mission on this earth as they listen to their lord who "tells them of His daily toil, of Edens newly made." [25] They are the "Strong Men" who "take their mirth in the joy of the Earth" and are fully aware of God's Law: "They know of toil and the end of toil." Kipling thus gives poetical expression to his activism and the divine law.

From this point of view, "McAndrew's Hymn" is one of Kipling's most significant poems which has a bearing on his world of values. It is a hymn of marine engines and other mechanical devices of a steamer: "What I ha' seen since ocean-steam began/Leaves me na doot for the machine: but what about the man?" Kipling's praise of the machine grows into a lovely symphony and achieves a universal significance. He declares that God has made the world "below the shadow of a dream" and he observes the hand of God in all things and "predestination in the stride o' yon connectin'-rod." [26] "McAndrew's Hymn" thus becomes the combination of the real and the ideal. To me it seems an excellent poetical expression of realism in art. Kipling is almost prophetic in visualizing the mutually contributory relationship between poetry and science which has become a hallmark of modern British and American poetry. The discoveries and inventions of science become objective realities of human experience and they, touched by the poet's imagination, are transformed into art. In this way "McAndrew's Hymn" becomes a masterpiece of Kipling's realism. Charles Eliot Norton, writing in 1897, had asked a pertinent question regarding "McAndrew's Hymn." "Mr. McAndrew, don't you think steam spoils romance at sea?" [27] The answer is a firm negative because the poet's imagination in "McAndrew's Hymn" bodies forth new forms and newer areas of experience. And Kipling in this regard follows the footsteps of Wordsworth who believed that poetry is "the impassioned expression which is in the countenance of all science" and the "breath and finer spirit of all knowledge." Kipling's approach to machines and technology, therefore, is very appreciative and positive because, like other nineteenth-century poets and thinkers, especially Walt Whitman, Kipling liked to accommodate science and technology to the vision within.

Yet, in spite of this affirmative and positive artistic vision, Kipling could not transcend a certain amount of moral ambivalence which is particularly evident in his myth of the Empire. Apparently at least, it is a dichotomous, almost dual, vision containing "the voice of the hooligan" and the vision of the moralist. As William Dean Howells has perceptively pointed out, Kipling's "patriotism is not love of the little England" [28] encompassed by the inviolate seas but the great England which becomes the focal center of sublimity, progress, and a mystical unity. An American, by virtue of being what he is, a citizen of the new world, cannot fully share Kipling's feeling for the Empire particularly because America broke away from the "little" England and the particular strand of her tradition. But it must be realized that had there been no British India and no British America, as colonial powers, there would have been no feeders to British Imperialism and consequently no real sources for the functioning of the Imperialistic Imagination. (I use this term in the context in which Lionel Trilling has used the term "Liberal Imagination" which is obviously an opposite.) And the fact of history, that the United States broke away from Great Britain, indirectly strengthened the feeling of imperialism in England of which Kipling is one of the products. However, the disillusionment with the Empire is much stronger in Kipling than the sense of pride in imperial possessions. Thus he unconsciously confirms the disillusionment of the Americans with the British power, shown at the time of the War of Independence, and anticipates the even more bitter disillusionment of Indians with the British power, resulting in India's independence in 1947. It is in this curious context that Howells claims that "Mr. Kipling, whether he likes it or not, is in some sort American." [29] Perhaps on a similar hypothesis it will be more justifiable to claim Kipling as an Indian because he was born in India, and also because legally he was an Anglo-Indian.

But the fact remains that Kipling's mystique of the Empire resulted in some of the finest poems depicting the average British soldier's life. No other English poet in the nineteenth and twentieth centuries has given such subtle expression of the British soldier's sense of community and companionship as Kipling. "Tommy" is his favorite character and in this poem he expresses with concrete precision and utmost empathy the personal problems and predicaments of the common soldier. Similarly "Danny Deever" is a spirited poem. Highly realistic, it is neither deeply melancholic nor disturbingly conscientious. The sorrowful note is struck, however, when the "whimpers over'ead" [30] is described as the passing of Danny's soul. The poem is sensitively rhythmic and deeply moving—qualities which made it highly popular among British servicemen all over the world. Thus Kipling has not only immortalized the British soldier in verse but also, as W. L. Renwick has pointed out,[31] vitalized the average Englishman's consciousness of himself and his world.

In spite of this idealization of the average British soldier, Kipling does not seem to really transcend the peculiar prejudices of the British. Consequently his soldier poems have a ring of condescension rooted in Kipling's awareness of himself as a Britisher. As George Orwell has pointed out, "if one examines his best and most representative work, his soldier poems, especially *Barrack-Room Ballads*, one notices that what more than anything else spoils them is an underlying air of patronage." [32] It is this which does seem to vitiate, to a certain extent, the impact of Kipling's soldier poems.

The presence of these elements of condescension and patronage, coupled with his allegedly imperialistic stance, has rendered the task of placing Kipling in the main tradition of English poetry highly difficult. He is readily acknowledged as a good, second-rate poet and versifier, although critical opinion in late nineteenth-century England tended to give him a much higher status. T. S. Eliot estimates him as a "laureate without laurels" and a "neglected celebrity." [33] Yet he points out the lack of cohesion in Kipling's poetry and his immaturity as a poet. As an example, he cites Kipling's poems in *The Years Between*, which "no more hang together than the verses of a schoolboy." Yet, in T. S. Eliot's view, "Kipling is very nearly a great writer" because of his unconscious, though naïve, appeal to the common English-reading public. It is noteworthy that Eliot has used the words "verse" or "great verse" to describe Kipling's output. The implication is that a major portion of Kipling's poetical production is verse and that he wrote very little which can be legitimately described as poetry nourished by the imagination. George Orwell goes to the other extreme when he describes most of Kipling's verse as "so horribly vulgar that it gives one the same sensation as one gets from watching a third-rate music-hall performer reciting a third-rate jingle-song." Orwell's estimate of Kipling is one-sided, but his contention that Kipling wrote a great deal of what he terms as "good bad poetry" appears in part valid. A great deal of late nineteenth-century and early twentieth-century English poetry may be described as "good bad" poetry and therefore Kipling's compositions find their place in this uneven, unequal, and ambiguous setting. But, on the strength of his "good" poems, Kipling's place is secure among second-rate poets and first-rate versifiers of the period.

One important question, however, must be raised again, although it remains mostly unanswered. How can one explain Kipling's tremendous popularity as a poet in his own day? And, how can one relate it to his second-rate status as a poet? Kipling, as has already been suggested, never considered himself a poet of a small, select coterie but addressed his poems to a large audience. T. S. Eliot, who represents the modern English poet's point of view, considers this a failing since almost all modern poets have a very limited audience. The assumption has grown over the years that the more limited the audience of a poet, the higher will be the merit and quality of his poetry. This gulf between the great and the popular which is a hallmark of modern English poetry, was unknown in Kipling's day. T. S. Eliot in this context visualizes one hypothetical "Intelligent Man" who, in fact, does not exist, but "who would, all the same, be the true audience of the Artist." This "Intelligent Man" represents the selective taste in modern poetry. This new, selective taste in modern English poetry has gone against Kipling and the recognition of his status as a poet in modern criticism.

These adverse judgments apart, Kipling, in my view, is a really great writer of verse and a remarkable poet. Not enough recognition has been accorded to the exuberant vitality that he bequeathed to his characters in fiction and poetry. As a poet, he seems to me a genuine activist who is primarily concerned with presenting and interpreting life as a series of authentic, throbbing, human experiences. The bustling life of humanity is his theme and the scenes and situations are as varied as the clouds in the sky or the pebbles on the shore. His poetry demonstrates the creative process of transformation from the activist into the artist.

7

Kipling's Idiolect

Kipling's style or what one can call his special idiolect [1] is a singularly neglected aspect in the study of his art and technique. The same critical disagreements which mark the evaluation of the other areas of his achievement operate in this regard also. There is a tendency, for instance, to consider Kipling as a gifted storyteller, and also, simultaneously, as one whose style, "involves no discoveries in syntax or vocabulary," and whose "structure reveals nothing unusual." [2] Such critiques tend to overlook the fact that there is no intrinsic dichotomy between style and substance. They are mutually inseparable and the older view that form and content, manner and matter could be regarded as separate categories is no longer valid. Modern stylistics emphasize the inviolable unity of form and content implying thereby that "saying about a thing includes the thing said." The conventional, but confusing, distinction between describing a thing and the thing itself is today considered not only an erring, but also a highly misleading, oversimplification. If style is isolated from the content and is regarded as a separate entity the appreciation of which is not bound up with the other aspects of an author, it merely becomes an embellishment and not an integral part of the artist's total achievement.

Therefore, the modes of Kipling's narration and expression should not be isolated from his overall vision as an artist, his general philosophy and background. From this point of view, Kipling's style is an instrument geared to the expression of his activist stance as a writer. The critical assumption that Kipling is essentially an activist who, through the process of creative expression, is transformed into an artist is particularly relevant to the study of his use of language. As an activist he uses the English language as a powerful instrument to communicate the significance of *actio*. He assimilates the oracular structure of the biblical language and in accordance with his artistic needs, he molds it creatively to express the peculiarities of his characters and situations. Similarly, conditioned by his needs as a creative writer, he uses slang, cockney, and even Hindustani to catch the color, the rhythm, and the natural postures of his fictional characters and situations.

Since "activism" is Kipling's basic world view, the most significant quality of his style is its vitality. Stemming from this belief in action his style is marked by a sense of concretion and earthiness. It is this vitality which gives it many oracular features. This capacity to identify himself with the life of his time "without an irritable reaching out after facts" gives to Kipling's mode of expression a peculiar pungency and freshness. Many of Kipling's phrases and sentences have a concrete earthiness which invests them with enduring significance. Phrases such as "East is East, West is West," and "the White Man's burden" have assumed a powerful currency in the reservoir of the language of modern politicians throughout the English-speaking world. It proves that Kipling did not use or coin mere clichés, but concretized the intellectual and spiritual tendencies of his age in telling words and phrases.

This capacity to crystallize contemporary patterns of thought and life through the nucleus of a vital style is particularly meaningful in relation to its historical context. Kipling wrote at a time when "dilettante elegancies" of expression were fashionable. The decadent finesse of the authors of the "naughty nineties," particularly the stylistics of Walter Pater and of the *Yellow Book*, affected the literary atmosphere powerfully. It gave rise to a literature, pseudo-romantic in tone, which sapped the vitality of language. Kipling impinged on this decadent literary milieu with his activistic-creed instinct, with the vitality of a world outside little, insular England. He created "young Leviathans" (like the innocent Infant in "A Conference of the Powers") [3] in his Anglo-Indian world, endowing them with the vision of a brave new world.

Although Kipling avoided the decadent stylistics of his own day, in molding his own style he was undoubtedly influenced by some of the elements of the eighteenth-century essay and satire. This seems strange in a writer who distinctly belongs to the late nineteenth century. But in his prose fiction we find that the narrative, as in an essay, is objective; it is marked by a seriousness of tone and there is a clearly discernible moralistic stance. Even the syntax is a simple combination of short clauses which between them fully clarify the locale, the object, and the moral. Similarly, there is a formalism of manner, reminiscent of the eighteenth-century essay, which appears like a thin layer over Kipling's sentence patterns. The following mode of narration, for example, presenting Findlayson's anxieties over the safety of the bridge on the Ganges in "The Bridge-Builders" is typical:

> There were no excuses in his service. Government might listen, perhaps, but his own kind would judge him by his bridge, as that stood or fell. He went over it in his head plate by plate, span by span, brick by brick, pier by pier, remembering, comparing, estimating, and recalculating, lest there should be any mistake; and through the long hours and through the flights of formulae that danced and wheeled before him a cold fear would come to pinch his heart.[4]

Here, Kipling's narrative pattern is simple, but the details of the bridge hovering in Findlayson's mind are structured and stylized as parts or points of an essay. The clauses are so constituted as to objectify the smallest detail in relation to Findlayson's mind. The operative process of his reasoning is unfolded before the reader's eye clearly and effectively. Thus the triumph here is one of sheer stylistics.

Similarly, in the story of the love affair of Wressley in "Wressley of the Foreign Office" Kipling's description of the young man's efforts to write his *"magnum opus"* – *"Native Rule in Central India"* – is peculiarly ironic, an irony characteristic of the eighteenth-century essayists. Wressley took one year's leave and worked hard on his project:

> Heavens, how that man worked! He caught his Rajahs, analysed his Rajahs, and traced them up into the mists of Time and beyond, with their queens and their concubines. He dated and cross-dated, pedigreed and triple-pedigreed, compared, noted, connoted, wove, strung, sorted, selected, inferred, calendared and counter-calendared for ten hours a day. And, because this sudden and new light of Love was upon him, he turned those dry bones of history and dirty records of misdeeds into things to weep or to laugh over as he pleased. His heart and soul were at the end of his pen, and they got into the ink. He was dowered with sympathy, insight, humour, and style for two hundred and thirty days and nights; and his book was a Book.[5]

This is an excellent example of the peculiar irony which marks Kipling's description of Wressley's endeavor to write. This futile effort is rounded off by making Miss Venner, Wressley's love, declare that she read his book, but "It's all about those howwid Wajahs. I didn't understand it."

Kipling's style is sometimes a fusion, as shown above, of the eighteenth-century essay and satire. But neither is it uniform nor has it an invariably single pattern or tune. His prose and verse show a mixed style and varied modes of narration and description, depending on the contextual need and relevance. While Kipling is capable of long, but skillfully written, passages of description, he is also good in what may be called "telegraphic style." His scenic descriptions tend to become impressionistic, each clause in a sentence or short sentences evoking a single, unified impression. This effect is a result of an extremely compressed style which characterizes Kipling's later work. Here Kipling shows real maturity in achieving a sense of economy. Even in some of the earlier work, such as "Tomlinson" (1891), Kipling shows unerring instinct for precision and lucidity, for the apt phrase and suggestive image. Tomlinson hears "the roar of the Milky Way," and in face of St. Peter's question on moral action, his "naked soul" grows "white as a rain-washed bone." [6] This image of the naked soul is singularly appropriate and meaningful. In conceiving and transmitting such images Kipling's style achieves a new dimension.

But the most significant, though highly controversial, dimension of Kipling's style is its extensive use of the Hindi or Hindustani dialect. *Kim, Plain Tales from the Hills,* and several other stories with an Indian background are full of Hindustani expressions. Sometimes the use of these Indian words is so extensive that it is highly baffling to a non-Indian reader. For instance, the following passage from "The Three Musketeers" in *Plain Tales from the Hills* is typical. In this story, Mulvaney, Learoyd, and Ortheris, the three musketeers, manage to abduct Lord Benira Trig in order to save an extra parade for the Regiment:

> Learoyd shows him wan down the sthreet, an' he sez, "How thruly Orientil! I will ride on a *hekka.*" I saw thin that our Rigimintal Saint was for givin' Thrigg over to us neck an' brisket. I purshued a *hekka,* an' I sez to the dhriver-divil, I sez, "Ye black limb, there's a *Sahib* comin' for this *hekka.* He wants to go *jildi* to the Padsahi Jhil"— 'twas about tu moiles away—"to shoot snipe—*chirria.* You dhrive *Jehannum ke marfik, mallum*— like Hell? 'Tis no manner av use *bukkin'* to the *Sahib,* bekase he doesn't *samjao* your talk. Av he *bolos* anything, just you *choop* and *chel. Dekker?* Go *arsty* for the first *arder* mile from contonmints. Thin *chel, Shaitan ke marfik,* an' the *chooper* you *choops* an' the *jildier* you *chels* the better *kooshy* will that Sahib be; an' here's a rupee for ye." [7]

The passage, as one can readily see, is full of native words: *hekka* is a horse-drawn carriage; "You dhrive *Jehannum ke marfik, mallum*" means "you should drive fast like Hell." The remark that *Sahib* "doesn't *samjao* [understand] your talk," is ironic since many of Kipling's non-Indian readers would be in a similar predicament. "Av he *bolos* [speaks] anything, just you *choop* [keep quiet] and *chel* [go ahead]" is another difficult sentence containing the native dialect vulgarized and distorted by local Englishmen. Grammatically, the local *Sahib* is anglicizing the Hindustani expressions; for instance *bolos* is used as a verb, in the present tense and indicative mood, as an equivalent of "says." Similarly, *bolo* is turned into *bolos,* *choop* is turned into *choops* and *chel* is transformed into *chels* in accordance with English usage. The English grammatical rules regarding comparative degree are also made applicable to Hindustani words as, for example, *jildi* (quick) becomes *jildier* (quicker) and "the better *kooshy* [pleased] will that Sahib be." This admixture of Hindustani words and rules of English usage is a peculiarity of the Anglo-Indian slang in Kipling's day. This resulted in some hybrid constructions which characterize Kipling's idiolect in his Anglo-Indian fiction.

These hybrid constructions and the use of Hindustani syntax have grated on the ears of many critics who regarded them as a major fault of Kipling's style. Expressing the typical American response to Kipling's use of the dialect, Clement M. Bellairs has unequivocally stated that its "greatest fault is the interlarding of English and Hindoostanee words and expressions." [8] Bellairs feels that this becomes a real barrier for an understanding of Kipling's stories, such as *The Story of the Gadsbys,*[9] which make an extensive use of Hindustani dialect. But, apart from other implications, the fact has to be noted that the language of the British civil servant in India had a peculiar identity of its own with its admixture of Victorian English and Hindustani words. Since Kipling was portraying the life of this class, he had to make use of the dialect which gives it its peculiar identity. This aspect probably has not been adequately appreciated by American critics partly because there is indeed no class in American society which can be equated with the British civil service in India of Kipling's days.

But the use of an alien dialect by itself does not interpose a barrier. The use of an alien dialect can be both a genuine source of authenticity and vitality and a dangerous source of distraction. Dennis Duffy, for instance, in his discussion of Kipling's use of the Indian dialect raises this question and asks pertinently: "Is not dialect a naive device for adding verisimilitude to work?" [10] But the naïveté does not cling to a dialect as such; it only depends on the artist's intention.

Kipling's use of the lingo of the Indian is not actuated by the desire to parade his knowledge of the alien tongue. In fact, though Kipling was born in India and learnt to speak Hindi first and English later, he is hostile to those who use native language merely for ostentation. He also satirizes the Indians who use English only to show off. For instance, the Bengali Babu Hurree Chunder Mookerjee in *Kim* is a special object of Kipling's satire. The Bengali Babu's pronunciation, his emphasis on long vowels, his peculiarities of pedantic English usage are skillfully brought out in the story. Words such as "opeenion," [11] "releegions," "offeecially," and "verree easy" show the Babu's peculiarities of pronunciation, and phrases like "all raight" and "de-Englished" convey a similar impression. Kipling describes Hurree Chunder Mookerjee talking to Kim about his English. Kim tells the Babu: "We must not be heard talking English here." The Babu replies rather jauntily, "That is all raight. I am only a Babu showing off my English to you. All we Babus talk English to show off." [12] The Babu speaks English to show off, but in *Kim* Kipling's intentions are quite the opposite, that is, to expose and ridicule the Babu's ways of expression.

Therefore, Kipling's use of native dialect is not conditioned by any extraneous factors other than aesthetic. The main intention is to create an effect of actuality and verisimilitude. As an artist, Kipling knows that he has to catch the reality and rhythm of the British in India which will make his characters lifelike and genuinely individual. Since the novelist has to present his characters without his own intervention, he has to fail back on the language which will reveal individual idiosyncracies. To render the speech of the character in the third-person narrative style is to rob the character of its individuality. It is this aesthetic criterion which accounts for Kipling's extensive use of Hindustani. For instance, the speech patterns of Kim and the lama are highly individual-istic and their nuances can be conveyed only through a direct and accurate report of the words they actually speak.

Kim and the lama are about to begin their railroad journey and the boy speaks to the holy man. " 'Ten thousand blessings,' shrilled Kim. 'O Holy One, a woman has given us in charity so that I can come with thee—a woman with a golden heart. I run for the *tikkut*.' " [13] Kim's language has an oriental touch; it is marked by his life-style; it is a reflection of his idealism and his down-to-earth sense. The lama's language on the other hand is peculiarly airy, ethereal and abstract, although it appears to seek the reality of the human spirit. "It is manifest that from time to time I shall acquire merit—if before that I have not found my River—by assuring myself that thy feet are set on wisdom." The lama describes the curator of the Lahore Museum as "a Fountain of Wisdom." In the last scene of the novel the lama describes his dark night of the soul: "The boat of my soul lacked direction." [14] This phraseology is typically Indian and is a true reflection of the Indian's speech patterns and poetic use of language.

Moreover, another basic motivation of Kipling's pervasive use of Hindustani words or their Anglicized form is to project the in-group responses of the British in India. The British sense of belonging to a group or a select community chosen by God to perform a civilizing mission on earth is a constantly recurring pattern in Kipling's fiction. The English in India find themselves a small community closely knit by their group ideals quite distinct from the larger mass of native Indians. Kipling's intention was to express their life-style, and this he could do only by using their language which is a mixture of English and Anglicized Hindustani. Style thus becomes an integral part of their life itself and reveals the innermost recesses of their mind. As Dennis Duffy has pointed out, in Kipling's style the mixed sentence patterns and hybrid constructions are not gratuitous efforts to lend his tales an exotic color; they are aesthetic modes to communicate the complex mores of a society compounded of groups and tribal segments. Kipling's idiolect aims at finding correlatives, in the concretions of words, phrases, and images, for this tribal consciousness.

These controversies apart, Kipling's idiolect is distinctively his own. It is highly individualistic since it is an expression of his artistic needs and compulsions. It is almost unique because there is no other comparable English writer in later-Victorian literature who can be described as the true interpreter of Anglo-India. More than this, he is, like Dickens in a different context, the artistic reporter of the Imperial England for posterity. He has endowed this "great England" with verisimilitude and vitality, and his idiolect remains the chief instrument in evoking that vitality.

Notes

1 – Life and Literary Reputation

1. Andrew Lang, "*Causerie*: 'At the Sign of the Ship,'" *Longman's Magazine*, 8 (Oct. 1886), 675–76.
2. "Novels and Stories," rev. of *Plain Tales from the Hills*, by Rudyard Kipling, *Saturday Review*, 65, No. 1702, 9 June 1888, 697–98.
3. Andrew Lang, rev. of *Plain Tales from the Hills*, by Rudyard Kipling, *Daily News* (London), 2 November 1889, p. 6.
4. Quoted from *The Letters of Henry James*, ed. Percy Lubbock (New York, 1920), by Charles E. Carrington in *Rudyard Kipling: His Life and Work*, p. 188.
5. Ibid., p. 193.
6. Extract from a letter by Robert Louis Stevenson, from the Tusitala Edition of Stevenson's works, *Letters*, 34 (London, 1924), p. 45. Both Stevenson and Kipling were very popular writers of their times.
7. This article, "Mr. Kipling's Writings," was first published anonymously in the *Times* (London), 25 March 1890. Later the editor of the *Times Literary Supplement* informed Roger L. Green that it was written by Thomas Humphrey Ward. See *Kipling*, ed. Roger L. Green, p. 50.
8. Carrington, *Rudyard Kipling*, p. 331.
9. Charles Morgan, *The House of Macmillan: 1843–1943* (New York, 1944), p. 151.
10. Robert Buchanan, *The Voice of "The Hooligan": A Discussion of Kiplingism* (New York, 1900), reprinted in abridged form in *Kipling and the Critics*, ed. Elliot L. Gilbert, pp. 20–32.
11. T. S. Eliot, ed., *A Choice of Kipling's Verse*.
12. T. S. Eliot, "Rudyard Kipling," in *On Poetry and Poets* (New York: Farrar, Straus & Giroux, 1957), p. 281.

13. H. E. Bates, *The Modern Short Story: A Critical Survey* (London, 1943), pp. 111–17.

14. Thomas N. Cross, "Rudyard Kipling's Sense of Identity," *Michigan Quarterly Review*, pp. 247–53.

15. "Baa Baa, Black Sheep," in *Kipling: Short Stories Selected and Introduced by Edward Parone* (New York: Dell, 1960), pp. 218–19.

16. Rudyard Kipling, *Something of Myself*, p. 9.

17. H. L. Varley, "Imperialism and Rudyard Kipling," *Journal of the History of Ideas*, p. 127.

18. J. P. Collins, "Rudyard Kipling at Lahore," *Nineteenth Century and After*, p. 82.

19. Louis L. Cornell, *Kipling in India*, p. 58.

20. *Rudyard Kipling's Writings in Prose and Verse*, Outward Bound edition (New York: Charles Scribner's Sons [c. 1897–c. 1937]), p. 74.

21. *Statesman* (New Delhi), 19 January 1936, p. 8.

22. M. R. Dua, "Rudyard Kipling as a Journalist," *Journalism Quarterly*, p. 116.

23. Collins, "Rudyard Kipling at Lahore," p. 88.

24. Thomas R. Henn, *Kipling* (New York: Barnes & Noble, Inc., 1967), p. 3.

25. Cross, "Rudyard Kipling's Sense of Identity," p. 251.

26. Howard C. Rice, *Rudyard Kipling in New England*, p. 29. Reprinted from the *New England Quarterly*, 9, No. 3 (Sept. 1936).

27. Frederick F. Van de Water, *Rudyard Kipling's Vermont Feud*, p. 89.

28. Cross, "Rudyard Kipling's Sense of Identity," p. 253.

2—Alienated Activist and Imperialist

1. E. San Juan, Jr., "The Question of Values in Victorian Activism," *Personalist*, pp. 41–59. He discusses the "individual styles of action" of William Earnest Henley (1849–1903), Rudyard Kipling (1865–1936), and Robert Louis Stevenson (1850–94) to demonstrate their identical attitudes to problems of destiny. He suggests that the essential moral problem centers on biography and is basically personal; that it is for man to change from a passive to an active role so that he should not be a mere floating body in the swift current of life, but one who would direct and control the current.

In another perceptive essay E. San Juan, Jr. has said that *Virtu* is the Renaissance word for excellent work. The Victorian activists recognized the importance and value of *Virtu* in their search for perfection of self. See "Toward a Definition of Victorian Activism," *Studies in English Literature, 1500–1900*, pp. 583–600.

2. Thomas Carlyle, *Sartor Resartus* (Bombay, 1944), p. 174.

3. Ibid., p. 178.

4. Ibid., p. 205.

5. A. M. D. Hughes, *Carlyle* (Oxford, 1957), p. 91.

6. "Recessional," in *A Choice of Kipling's Verse*, ed. T. S. Eliot, p. 140.

7. "Gentlemen-Rankers," in *A Choice of Kipling's Verse*, p. 194.

8. Ibid., p. 193.

9. "The Galley-Slave," in *Departmental Ditties*, p. 156.

10. "The Glory of the Garden," in *Sixty Poems*, p. 39.

11. "My New-Cut Ashlar," in *Sixty Poems*, p. 7.

12. *Contemporary Review*, 76, No. 774 (Dec. 1899), quoted by H. L. Varley in "Imperialism and Rudyard Kipling," *Journal of the History of Ideas*, p. 125.

13. Wilhelm Dening, "Rudyard Kipling im heutigen englischen Unterricht," *Die Neueren Sprachen*, 48, Nos. 10–11 (1940), 192–93.

14. Hannah Arendt, "The Imperialist Character," *Review of Politics*, pp. 303–20.

15. H. E. Bates, *The Modern Short Story: A Critical Survey* (London, 1943), pp. 111–17.

16. Nelson Sherwin Bushnell, *The Historical Background of English Literature* (New York, 1930), pp. 308–10.

17. Charles E. Carrington, "Kipling and the Empire," *Kipling Journal* 29, No. 141 (March 1962), 8.

18. Bonamy Dobrée, *Rudyard Kipling*, p. 44.

19. The Great Uprising of 1857 in India (Indian Mutiny, 1857–58), also called the Sepoy Rebellion, resulted primarily from the discontent of Indian soldiers of the East India Company, which ruled India at that time. Their discontent was due to various causes, such as the use of cartridges greased with cow and pig fat, which offended the religious susceptibilities of Hindus and Muslims, and the people's resentment of the British annexation of several Indian states. This rebellion was finally overcome by the British, resulting in the assumption of direct responsibility by the British Crown.

20. Donald C. Gordon, *The Moment of Power: Britain's Imperial Epoch* (Englewood Cliffs, N.J.: Prentice-Hall 1970), p. 123.

21. "The First Sailor," in *A Book of Words*, p. 22.

22. "The Tomb of His Ancestors," in *The Day's Work*, pp. 118–19.

23. "The Song of the Dead," in *Sixty Poems*, p. 17.

24. "Arithmetic On the Frontier," in *Departmental Ditties*, p. 96.

25. J. I. M. Stewart, *Rudyard Kipling* (New York: Dodd, Mead & Co., 1966), p. 180.

26. Dobrée, *Rudyard Kipling*, p. 84.

27. G. N. Curzon, "The True Imperialism," *Nineteenth Century* (Jan. 1908), quoted by A. P. Thornton in *The Imperial Idea and Its Enemies: A Study in British Power* (New York: Doubleday, Anchor Books, 1968), p. 82.

28. Jawharlal Nehru, *An Autobiography* (London, 1936), p. 428.

29. "The Maltese Cat," in *The Day's Work*, p. 201.

30. Ibid.

3 – Kim

1. Mark Kinkead-Weekes, "Vision in Kipling's Novels," in *Kipling's Mind and Art*, ed. Andrew Rutherford, p. 217.

2. Nirad C. Chaudhuri, "The Finest Story About India — in English," *Encounter*, 13, No. 4 (April 1957), 48.

3. Review of *Kim*, *Athenaeum*, 118, 26 October 1901, 553.

4. Review of *Kim*, *Saturday Review*, 92, 12 October 1901, 461.

5. Review of *Kim*, *Westminster Review*, 156 (Dec. 1901), 711.

6. Review of *Kim*, *Literature*, 9, 5 October 1901, 326.

7. J. H. Millar, "Kim," *Blackwood's Magazine*, 170 (Dec. 1901), 795.

8. Edmund Wilson, "The Kipling that Nobody Read," reprinted from *The Wound and the Bow* (1952), in *Kipling's Mind and Art*, ed. Andrew Rutherford, p. 30.

9. A. B. Maurice's comment on *Kim* is quoted by Thomas R. Henn in *Kipling* (New York, Barnes & Noble Inc., 1967), p. 94.

10. T. S. Eliot, "An Essay on Rudyard Kipling," in *A Choice of Kipling's Verse*, p. 30.

11. Boris Ford, "A Case for Kipling," reprinted from *Scru-*

tiny, 11, No. 1 (1942), in *Kipling and the Critics*, ed. Elliot L. Gilbert, p. 61.

12. *Kim*, p. 305.

13. Ibid., p. 202.

14. Ibid.

15. Ibid., p. 292.

16. *Ananda*. One of the chief early disciples of the Buddha. Ananda was Buddha's first cousin and extremely devoted to him. The Buddha before his death spoke of Ananda in glowing terms (in the form of a panegyric). Ananda was a very lovable and sincere person and took a prominent part in Buddhistic councils.

17. *Kim*, p. 21.

18. Ibid., p. 68.

19. Ibid., p. 135.

20. *Stupas*. Stupa (Sanskrit), a Buddhist monument or mausoleum, generally called "tope" (from Pali *thupa*) in India, means "mound." The stupa was built in the shape of a tower, surmounted by a cupola. King Ashokais is said to have built 84,000 stupas in different parts of India in the third century B.C.

21. *Viharas*. A Buddhist monastery or temple with large grounds occupies an important position in the architectural glories of the Buddhist religion. The Buddhist *Sadhakas* resided in *Viharas*.

22. *Kim*, pp. 119–20.

23. Ibid., p. 123.

24. Ibid., p. 134.

25. Ibid., p. 9.

26. Ibid., pp. 174–75.

27. Quoted from *The Teachings of the Compassionate Buddha*, ed., with commentary, E. A. Burtt (New York: New American Library, Mentor Books, 1955), p. 156.

28. *Hinayana* (Little Vehicle). The disciple in this school of southern Buddhism aims at becoming an *arahat* (a private Buddha or *pratyekabuddha*), i.e., one who attains the Truths independently and does not preach.

29. *Mahayana* (Great Vehicle). The Great Vehicle is that each individual should aim not at attaining *Nirvana* only for himself but that he should train himself to become a Buddha and thus save a great many of his fellow sufferers in this world.

30. Tantric School of Buddhism. The Tantras are the religious textbooks of the *Shaktas* and of their various sects. There are different Tantric Schools, with variant traditions. Buddhist Tantrism would include the description and the history of its rites,

its deities, and its doctrines. Tantrism would cover "therugi," a highly developed mysticism styled *Vajrayana,* as well as many magical rites.

31. Agehananda Bharati, *The Tantric Tradition* (New York: Doubleday, Anchor Books, 1970), p. 15.

32. *Bodhisat.* This word is derived from "Bodhisattva," meaning one who is destined to gain supreme wisdom, on the way to Buddhahood but not yet perfectly enlightened. Etymologically, it means "one whose essence is perfect knowledge."

33. *Nirvana* (Sanskrit; Pali, *Nabbana*). The word in Sanskrit means "a blowing out," as in the case of a candle. This does not imply annihilation of personality, rather, the blowing out of desire which is the cause and effect of reincarnation, the cycle of birth and death. This is the end of the road of existences, the extinction of *Karma* and the coming of a state of blessedness.

34. *Kim,* pp. 311–12.

4—Minor Fiction

1. Joyce M. S. Tompkins, *The Art of Rudyard Kipling,* p. 2.
2. Thomas R. Henn, *Kipling* (New York: Barnes & Noble, Inc., 1967), pp. 88–92.
3. Mark Kinkead-Weekes, "Vision in Kipling's Novels," in *Kipling's Mind and Art,* ed. Andrew Rutherford, p. 211.
4. *Captains Courageous,* p. 13.
5. Ibid., p. 173.
6. Ibid., pp. 125–26.
7. Rudyard Kipling, *Something of Myself,* p. 6.
8. "Baa Baa, Black Sheep," in *Kipling: Short Stories Selected and Introduced by Edward Parone* (New York: Dell Publishing Co., 1960), p. 219.
9. *The Light that Failed,* p. 10.
10. Tompkins, *The Art of Rudyard Kipling,* p. 10.
11. Eric Solomon, "*The Light that Failed* as a War Novel," *English Fiction in Transition,* 5 (1962), 30.
12. C. M. G. Masterman, *In Peril of Change* (London, 1905), p. 7.
13. *The Light that Failed,* p. 17.
14. Ibid., p. 23.
15. Ibid., p. 29.
16. Henn, *Kipling,* pp. 80–81.

5 – Short Stories

1. Andrew Lang, "Mr. Kipling's Stories," in *Essays in Little* (London, 1891), pp. 198–205, reprinted in *Kipling*, ed. Roger L. Green, p. 71.

2. Originally published as an anonymous review of *Plain Tales from the Hills*, by Rudyard Kipling (London and Calcutta: Thacker and Spink, 1888) in the *Saturday Review*, 65, No. 1702, 9 June 1888, 697–98, under the title "Novels and Stories." Later it was known that the review was written by the editor of the *Saturday Review*, Walter Herries Pollock (1850–1926). See the reference in *Kipling*, ed. Roger L. Green, p. 37.

3. Edmund Gosse, "Rudyard Kipling," *Century Magazine*, 42 (Oct. 1891), 904–5.

4. G. K. Chesterton rev. of *Just So Stories*, by Rudyard Kipling, *Bookman* (London), 23 (Nov. 1902), 57–58.

5. Joyce M. S. Tompkins, *The Art of Rudyard Kipling*.

6. C. A. Bodelsen, *Aspects of Rudyard Kipling's Art*.

7. Randall Jarrell, "On Preparing to Read Kipling," in *A Sad Heart at the Supermarket* (New York: Atheneum, 1962), pp. 114–39. It was earlier published as the introduction to *The Best Short Stories of Rudyard Kipling*, ed. Randall Jarrell (New York: Doubleday, 1961).

8. "The Bridge-Builders," in *The Day's Work*, p. 7.

9. Ibid., p. 13.

10. Ibid., p. 30.

11. Tompkins, *The Art of Rudyard Kipling*, p. 191.

12. "The Bridge-Builders," p. 38.

13. "The Miracle of Purun Bhagat," in *The Second Jungle Book*, p. 27.

14. Ibid., p. 28.

15. Ibid., p. 31.

16. Tompkins, *The Art of Rudyard Kipling*, p. 56.

17. K. R. Srinivasa Iyengar, "Kipling's Indian Tales," in *The Image of India in Western Creative Writing*, ed. M. K. Naik (Madras, India: 1971), p. 80.

18. "Without Benefit of Clergy," in *The Mark of the Beast and Other Stories*, ed. Roger Burlingame (New York: New American Library, Signet Classic, 1964), p. 29.

19. Elliot L. Gilbert, "Without Benefit of Clergy: A Farewell to Ritual," *Kipling and the Critics*, p. 33.

20. "The Story of Muhammed Din," in *Plain Tales from the Hills*, p. 230.

21. E. M. Forster, *Where Angels Fear to Tread* (New York: Random House, Vintage Books, 1958), p. 140.

22. K. Bhaskara Rao, *Rudyard Kipling's India*, p. 50.

23. "The Brushwood Boy," in *The Mark of the Beast and Other Stories*, p. 86.

24. Ibid., p. 112.

25. "The Gardner," in *The Mark of the Beast and Other Stories*, p. 341.

26. Ibid., p. 350.

27. Rudyard Kipling, *Something of Myself*, p. 208.

28. Rudyard Kipling was enrolled as a member of the Masonic Lodge in Lahore in 1885. He was also later associated with the founding of the Masonic Lodges of the Imperial War Graves Commission. See *Kipling Journal*, No. 31 (Sept. 1934), p. 76.

29. Thomas R. Henn, *Kipling* (New York: Barnes & Noble, Inc., 1967), p. 28.

30. "The Phantom 'Rickshaw," in *Kipling: Short Stories Selected and Introduced by Edward Parone* (New York: Dell Publishing Co., 1960), p. 34.

31. "A Wayside Comedy," in *Wee Willie Winkie*, p. 42.

32. Louis L. Cornell, *Kipling in India*, p. 161.

33. Bonamy Dobrée, *Rudyard Kipling*, p. 29.

34. Elsie B. Adams, "No Exit: An Explication of Kipling's 'A Wayside Comedy,' " *English Literature in Transition*, II, No. 3 (1968), 180–83.

35. C. A. Bodelsen, "Two Enigmatic Kipling Stories: An Interpretation of 'The Prophet and the Country' and 'Mrs. Bathurst,' " *Orbis Litterarum*, 16 (Copenhagen, 1961), 3–26.

36. P. W. Brock, " 'Mrs. Bathurst': A Final Summing Up," *Kipling Journal*, No. 31 (Sept. 1964), pp. 6–10.

6–Poetry

1. Bonamy Dobrée, *Rudyard Kipling*, pp. 203–8. Professor Dobrée has coined a new term to suggest a kind of poetry written in "a style, a language, which, rather than inviting the imagination to roam, concentrates it on our half-apprehended intuitions." In his view Kipling wrote a great deal of "actuality poetry" in his later phase. Wallace Stevens is a more recent practitioner of this kind of poetry.

2. Roger Burlingame, "Foreword," in *The Mark of the Beast*

and Other Stories (New York: New American Library, Signet Classic, 1964), p. ix.

3. Lionel Stevenson, "The Ideas in Kipling's Poetry," *University of Toronto Quarterly*, p. 468.

4. T. S. Eliot, "Swinburne as Poet," in *The Sacred Wood: Essays on Poetry and Criticism* (London, 1920), p. 146. T. S. Eliot commenting on Swinburne's poetry writes, "I am inclined to think that the word 'beauty' is hardly to be used in connection with Swinburne's verse at all, but in any case the beauty or effect of sound is neither that of music nor that of poetry which can be set to music."

5. "The Ballad of East and West," in *Sixty Poems*, p. 98.

6. Karl W. Deutsch and Norbert Wiener, "The Lonely Nationalism of Rudyard Kipling," *Yale Review*, 52, No. 4 (June 1963), 499–500.

7. See "Warburton, Colonel Sir Robert," *Encyclopedia Britannica*, 11th ed., Vol. 28, 1911.

8. This is a phrase used by J. M. Cohen in explaining Maurice Bowra's attitude to Robert Browning; see Cohen, *Robert Browning* (London: Longmans Green & Co., 1952), p. 181. A similar view is suggested in John Heath-Stubb's *The Darkling Plain: A Study of the Later Fortunes of Romanticism* (Folcroft, Pa., 1950).

9. "The Betrothed," in *Departmental Ditties*, p. 100.

10. "The Plea of the Simla Dancers," in *Departmental Ditties*, p. 109.

11. "An Old Song," in *Departmental Ditties*, p. 125.

12. "The Moon of Other Days," in *Departmental Ditties*, pp. 135–36.

13. *Sere Farash*. The head of heavens or of infinite space is associated in this context with the principle of imagination.

14. Hafiz. Pseudonym of Shams-ad-Din Mohammed (1320–89), Persian lyric poet, distinguished by his fresh and original poetical treatment of old romantic themes such as love and nature. He inspired many romantic poets of the nineteenth century, including Kipling.

15. "Certain Maxims of Hafiz," in *Departmental Ditties*, p. 130.

16. "To the Unknown Goddess," in *Departmental Ditties*, p. 48.

17. "My Rival," in *Departmental Ditties*, p. 45.

18. "The Lover's Litany," in *Departmental Ditties*, p. 63.

19. "As the Bell Clinks," in *Departmental Ditties*, p. 113.

20. Quoted by Edward Dowden in "The Poetry of Mr. Kipling," *New Literary Review*, 38 (Feb. 1901), 53–61, and reprinted in *Kipling*, ed. Roger L. Green, p. 263.

21. Robert Browning, "Fra Lippo Lippi," in *Men and Women*, ed. G. E. Hadow (Oxford, 1951), p. 136.

22. "Pagett, M.P.," in *Departmental Ditties*, p. 55.

23. "The Sons of Martha," in *A Choice of Kipling's Verse*, ed. T. S. Eliot, p. 159.

24. "The Secret of the Machines," in *A Choice of Kipling's Verse*, p. 294.

25. "Dedication from Barrack-Room Ballads," in *A Choice of Kipling's Verse*, p. 44.

26. "McAndrew's Hymn," in *A Choice of Kipling's Verse*, p. 57.

27. Charles Eliot Norton, "The Poetry of Rudyard Kipling," *Atlantic Monthly*, p. 115.

28. William Dean Howells, "The Laureate of the Larger England," *McClure's Magazine*, 8 (March 1897), 452.

29. Ibid., p. 453.

30. "Danny Deever," in *A Choice of Kipling's Verse*, p. 172. Although "Danny Deever" is considered "light verse" by W. H. Auden, its underlying tone is serious and, according to Bonamy Dobrée, it expresses the communal sense in the phrase "Files-on-Parade."

31. W. L. Renwick, "Re-reading Kipling," *Durham University Journal*, 32 (Jan. 1940), 3–16.

32. George Orwell, "Rudyard Kipling," in *Kipling's Mind and Art*, ed. Andrew Rutherford, p. 75.

33. T. S. Eliot, "Kipling Redivivus," *Athenaeum*, No. 4645, 9 May 1919, p. 297.

7—Kipling's Idiolect

1. *Idiolect.* Linguists have coined this new word for the peculiar use of language by a particular speaker. Every novelist or poet develops his own idiolect and this fact comes in the way of formulating a general theory of style. Nevertheless, certain modes of expression and use of language, with their peculiarities, will lead to the concept of the creative writer's especial idiolect. See *The Theory of the Novel*, ed. Philip Stevick (New York: Free Press, 1967), pp. 185–86.

2. T. S. Eliot, "Kipling Redivivus," *Athenaeum*, No. 4645, 9 May 1919, pp. 297–98.

3. "A Conference of the Powers," in *Many Inventions*. The narrator is entertaining army friends in his chambers in London, when Eustace Cleever comes in. The boys and Eustace exchange greetings, and the boys talk about their experiences, especially in Burma.

4. "The Bridge-Builders," in *The Day's Work*, p. 21.

5. "Wressley in the Foreign Office," in *Plain Tales from the Hills*, p. 240.

6. "Tomlinson," in *A Choice of Kipling's Verse*, ed. T. S. Eliot, pp. 146–47.

7. "The Three Musketeers," in *Plain Tales from the Hills*, p. 62.

8. Clement M. Bellairs, "Rudyard Kipling's Field," rev. *New York Times*, 14 December 1890, p. 5.

9. "The Story of the Gadsbys," in *Soldiers Three*.

10. Dennis Duffy, "Kipling and the Dialect of the Tribe," *Dalhousie Review*, p. 345.

11. *Kim*, p. 198.

12. Ibid., p. 200.

13. Ibid., p. 39.

14. Ibid., p. 311.

Selected Bibliography

Bibliographies

Lauterbach, Edward S. "An Annotated Bibliography of Writings about Rudyard Kipling." *English Literature in Transition,* 8, No. 3 (1960), 136–202; and 8, No. 4 (1960), 203–41.

Livingstone, Flora V. *Bibliography of the Works of Rudyard Kipling.* New York: Edgar H. Wells, 1927.

Martindell, Ernest W. *Bibliography of the Works of Rudyard Kipling, 1881–1923.* London: John Lane, 1923.

Handbooks and Dictionaries

Durand, Ralph. *A Handbook to the Poetry of Rudyard Kipling.* Garden City N.Y.: Doubleday & Co., 1914.

Young, Arthur W. Q. and McGivering, John H. *A Kipling Dictionary.* New York: St. Martin's Press, 1967.

Works by Kipling

Actions and Reactions. New York: Charles Scribner's Sons, 1913.

Barrack-Room Ballads. Garden City, N.Y.: Doubleday & Co., 1892.

A Book of Words: Selections from Speeches and Addresses Delivered between 1906–1927. New York: Charles Scribner's Sons, 1928.

Captains Courageous. New York: Dell Publishing Co., 1963.

The Day's Work. London: Macmillan & Co. Ltd., 1964.

Debits and Credits. New York: Charles Scribner's Sons, 1926.

Departmental Ditties. London: Methuen and Co., Dominions Edition, 1914.

A *Diversity of Creatures*, New York: Charles Scribner's Sons, 1917.

Early Verse. New York: Charles Scribner's Sons, 1913

From Sea to Sea: Letters of Travel, 1887–1889, 2 Vols. Garden City, N.Y.: Doubleday & Co., 1899.

The Jungle Book. New York: Charles Scribner's Sons, 1897.

Just So Stories For Little Children. London: Macmillan & Co. Ltd., 1962.

Kim. London: Macmillan & Co. Ltd., Papermac Edition, 1969.

Land Sea Tales for Boys and Girls. New York: Charles Scribner's Sons, 1937.

Letters of Travel: 1892–1913. New York: Charles Scribner's Sons, 1920.

Life's Handicap. Garden City, N.Y.: Doubleday & Co., 1923.

The Light that Failed. Harmondsworth, Eng.: Penguin Modern Classics, 1970.

Many Inventions. London: Macmillan & Co. Ltd., 1964.

Naulahka: A Story of West and East. New York: Charles Scribner's Sons, 1897.

Plain Tales from the Hills. London: Macmillan & Co. Ltd., 1964.

Puck of Pook's Hill. New York: Charles Scribner's Sons, 1913.

Rewards and Fairies. New York: Charles Scribner's Sons, 1916.

Rudyard Kipling's Verse. Definitive Edition. Garden City, N.Y.: Doubleday & Co., 1945.

The Second Jungle Book. New York: Charles Scribner's Sons, 1897.

Sixty Poems. London: Hodder and Stoughton, 1939.

Soldiers Three and Other Stories. London: Macmillan & Co. Ltd., 1964.

Something of Myself, For My Friends Known and Unknown. Garden City, N.Y.: Doubleday & Co., 1937.

Stalky and Co. London: Macmillan & Co. Ltd., 1962.

Traffics and Discoveries. New York: Charles Scribner's Sons, 1913.

Wee Willie Winkie and Other Stories. London: Macmillan & Co. Ltd., 1964.

The Years Between and Poems from History. New York: Charles Scribner's Sons, 1919.

Works on *Kipling*

BOOKS

Beresford, G. C. *Schooldays With Kipling.* New York: G. P. Putnam & Sons, 1936.

Bhaskar Rao, K. *Rudyard Kipling's India.* Norman, Okla.: University of Oklahoma Press, 1967.

Bodelsen, C. A. *Aspects of Rudyard Kipling's Art.* Manchester, Eng.: Manchester University Press, 1964.

Braybrooke, Patrick. *Kipling and His Soldiers.* Philadelphia: J. B. Lippincott, 1925.

Brown, Hilton. *Rudyard Kipling.* New York: Harper & Brothers, 1945

Carrington, Charles. *Rudyard Kipling: His Life and Work.* London: Macmillan and Co., 1955.

Cornell, Louis L. *Kipling in India.* New York: St. Martin's Press, 1966.

Croft-Cooke, Rupert. *Rudyard Kipling.* London: Home & Van Thal Ltd., 1948.

Dobrée, Bonamy. *Rudyard Kipling.* London: Longmans Green Ltd., 1951.

————. *Rudyard Kipling: Realist and Fabulist.* New York: Oxford University Press, 1967.

Eliot, T. S. *A Choice of Kipling's Verse made by T. S. Eliot with an Essay on Rudyard Kipling.* Originally published 1941. London: Faber and Faber, 1963.

Gilbert, Elliott L., ed. *Kipling and the Critics.* New York: New York University Press, Gotham Library, 1965.

Green, Roger L., ed. *Kipling: The Critical Heritage.* New York: Barnes & Noble, Inc., 1971.

Hart, Walter Morris. *Kipling the Story Writer.* Berkeley: University of California Press, 1918.

Hopkins, R. Thurston. *Rudyard Kipling: A Literary Appreciation.* New York: Frederick A. Stokes, Ltd., 1915.

Kipling, John Lockwood. *Beast and Man in India: A Popular Sketch of Indian Animals in their Relations with the People.* London: Macmillan & Co. Ltd., 1891.

The Kipling Journal. Issued by the Kipling Society, London, 1927–56.

Knowles, Frederick Lawrence. *A Kipling Primer.* Boston: Little, Brown, 1899.

Lawton, William Cranston. *Rudyard Kipling, the Artist: A Retrospect and a Prophecy.* New York: Morse, 1899.

Leáud François. *La Poétique de Rudyard Kipling.* Paris: Didier, 1958.

Maugham W. Somerset, ed. *A Choice of Kipling's Best.* Garden City, N.Y.: Doubleday, & Co. 1953.

Munson, Arley. *Kipling's India.* Garden City, N.Y.: Doubleday & Co., 1915.

Naik, M. K., ed. *The Image of India in Western Creative Writing.* Madras, India: Macmillan & Co. Ltd., 1970.

Palmer, John Leslie. *Rudyard Kipling.* London: Nisbett, 1915.

Parker, William B. *The Religion of Mr. Kipling.* New York: M. F. Mansfield & A. Wessels, 1899.

Rice, Howard C. *Rudyard Kipling in New England.* Brattleboro, Vt.: Stephen Daye Press, 1936.

Rutherford, A., ed. *Kipling's Mind and Art: Selected Critical Essays.* Stanford, Calif.: Stanford University Press, 1964.

Sajjad Hussain, S. *Kipling and India.* Dacca, Pak.: University of Dacca Press, 1963.

Shanks, Edward. *Rudyard Kipling. A Study in Literature and Political Ideas.* Garden City, N.Y.: Doubleday & Co., 1940.

Shen, Tsung-Lien. *Tibet and the Tibetans.* Stanford, Calif.: Stanford University Press, 1952.

Singh, Bhupal. *A Survey of Anglo-Indian Fiction.* London: Oxford University Press, 1934.

Tapp, Major H. A. *The United Services College, 1874–1911.* Portsmouth, Eng.: Gale & Polden, 1933.

Tompkins, J. M. S. *The Art of Rudyard Kipling. The Centenary Edition,* Lincoln: Nebraska University Press, 1965.

Trilling, Lionel. *The Liberal Imagination.* Garden City, N.Y.: Doubleday & Co., 1957.

Van De Water, Frederic F. *Rudyard Kipling's Vermont Feud.* New York: Reynal & Hitchcock, 1937.

Weygandt, Ann Matlack. *Kipling's Reading and Its Influence On His Poetry.* Philadelphia: University of Pennsylvania Press, 1939.

Williams, Jesse Lynch. *Rudyard Kipling.* New York: Charles Scribner's Sons, 1899.

Wilson, Edmund. *The Wound and the Bow.* Boston: Houghton Mifflin, 1941.

ARTICLES

Arendt, Hannah. "The Imperialist Character." *Review of Politics,* 12, No. 3 (1950), 303–20.

Barrie, James M. "Mr. Kipling's Stories." *Contemporary Review*, 59 (1891), 364–72.

Bhattacharjee, Mohinimohan. "Rudyard Kipling: An Appreciation." *Calcutta Review*, 59 (April–May 1936), 97–106, 177–89.

Chaudhuri, Nirad C. "Passage to and From India." *Encounter*, 2 (1954), 19–24.

Collins, J. P. "Rudyard Kipling at Lahore." *Nineteenth Century and After*, 121 (1937), 80–90.

Cook, Richard. "Rudyard Kipling and George Orwell." *Modern Fiction Studies*, 7 (1961), 125–35.

Cross, Thomas N. "Rudyard Kipling's Sense of Identity." *Michigan Quarterly Review*, 4, No. 4 (1965), 247–53.

Dobree, Bonamy. "Rudyard Kipling: A New Aspect." *Listener* (London). 47, 12 June 1952, 967–68.

Dua, M. R. "Rudyard Kipling as a Journalist: An Indian Evaluation." *Journalism Quarterly*, 45 (1968), 113–16.

Duffy, Dennis. "Kipling and the Dialect of His Time." *Dalhousie Review* (Halifax), 47, No. 3 (1967), 344–54.

Edwards, Michael. "Rudyard Kipling and the Imperial Imagination." *Twentieth Century*, 153 (1953), 443–54.

Forbes, Edgar Allen. "Across India with Kim." *World's Work*, 24 (1912), 639–49.

Krishnaswami, P. R. "Indian Characters in English Fiction." *Empire Review* (London), 43 (1926), 34–40.

Montgomery, M. "The Nationality of Kipling's Kim." *Germanische Romanische Monatschrift*, 6 (1914), 587–88.

Norton, Charles Eliot. "The Poetry of Rudyard Kipling." *Atlantic*, 79 (1897), 111–15.

Robinson, E. Kay. "Kipling in India." *McClure's*, 7 (1896), 99–109.

Roy, Sarath A. R. "Rudyard Kipling Seen Through Hindu Eyes." *North American Review*, 199 (1914), 271–81.

San Juan, Jr., E. "Toward a Definition of Victorian Activism." *Studies in English Literature 1500–1900*, 4, No. 4 (1964), 583–600.

———. "The Question of Values in Victorian Activism." *Personalist*, 45 (1964), 41–59.

Singh, Nihal. "Indians and Anglo-Indians: As Portrayed to Britons by British Novelists." *Modern Review*, 36 (1924), 251–56.

Stevenson, Lionel. "The Ideas in Kipling's Poetry." *University of Toronto Quarterly*, 1 (1932), 467–89.

Thompson, C. Patrick. "The White-faced Boy of Lahore." *World Review*, 8, 25 February 1929, 56–57.

Varley, Henry Leland. "Imperialism and Rudyard Kipling." *Journal of the History of Ideas*, 14 (1953), 124–25.

Waterhouse, Francis Asbury. "The Literary Fortunes of Kipling." *Yale Review*, 10 (1912), 817–31.

Index

Activism: defined, 22; and alienation, 22; in Victorian age, 22–23; and Herbert Spencer, 23; Kipling on, 26, 28–30, 40; in Tennyson's "Ulysses," 23–24; in "Locksley Hall," 24; in Carlyle, 24–25; and moral principle, 25; in "Recessional," 26; in "The Galley-Slave," 28, 117; in *Captains Courageous*, 71, 73; activist into artist, 71, 81, 88, 123; in Kipling's poetry, 116, 117, 123; and positivistic belief in progress, 117; in language, 124–25; as world view, 125

Adams, Elsie B., 104

Agehananda Bharati, 66

Alice in Wonderland, 96

Alienation: and activism, 22; in Kipling, 27; and "Gentlemen-Rankers," 27

Allen, Sir George: the chief of *Pioneer*, 14

Amir Abdul Rahman, 14

"An Old Song," 114

Arendt, Hannah: on Kipling's imperialism, 31

"Arithmetic on the Frontier," 36

"As the Bell Clinks," 116

"Ave Imperatix," 12

"Baa Baa, Black Sheep," 8–9, 75–76

Baldwin, Stanley, 7–8

Balestier, Beatty, 19–20

Balestier, Caroline: married to Rudyard, 18; voyage, 19; at Vermont, 19–20

Balestier, Wolcott: association with Kipling, 18

"Ballad of East and West, The": events misinterpreted, 110, 111; story of Warburton, 112; the theme, 112–13

Barrack-Room Ballads: published, 17; dedication, 118; air of patronage in, 121

Bates, H. E.: on imperialism, 31; mentioned, 6

"Bathurst, Mrs.": events in, 105–7

Beardsley, Aubrey, 21

Beerbohm, Max, 5, 80

Bellairs, Clement B.: on style, 129

Berg Collection, 16